51+ Fun Things To Do and Amazing Places To Visit in

MAUI

An Updated Pocket Travel Guide For Your Perfect Hawaiian Vacation With Outdoor Unmissable Activities, Local Tips and Must See Attractions

Alec James

Copyright © 2023 by Alec James

Acknowledgement and Disclaimer

We have invested substantial effort to ensure that this travel guide offers accurate and current information as of its publication date. Nevertheless, we acknowledge that some details such as contact details, operational hours, pricing, and travel information are susceptible to change. We cannot be held accountable for any inconveniences that may arise from the use of this guide or for the precision and appropriateness of information obtained from third-party sources.

We strongly urge readers to independently verify the information presented in this guide and to authenticate any specifics with the pertinent establishments or authorities prior to finalizing travel arrangements. Remain vigilant for any updates or alterations that may transpire subsequent to the publication of this guide.

Your safety and satisfaction are of paramount importance to us, and we greatly appreciate your comprehension of the dynamic nature of travel-related information. It is our hope that this guide enriches your journey and stands as a valuable resource throughout your travels.

Table of Contents

INTRODUCTION: WELCOME TO MAUI

Ah, Maui! The very name conjures images of swaying palm trees, crystalline waters, and sunsets that paint the sky in hues you never knew existed. You're about to embark on a journey to a place that's not just an island, but a living, breathing testament to nature's artistry.

As you step off the plane, a gentle breeze welcomes you, as if to say, "You're in Maui now, leave your worries at the door. It's a greeting unlike any other, a warm welcome from the natural world. I still remember my first visit here, a few years back. The air seemed to shimmer with anticipation, as if the island itself knew the adventure that awaited.

Maui is a place that wears many hats, and it wears them all well. Whether you're seeking the thrill of surfing the waves or the tranquillity of a quiet cove,

Maui obliges with open arms. Families build sandcastles alongside seasoned surfers, sharing the shoreline in harmony.

Now, let's address the age-old debate: sunrise or sunset at Haleakalā? Allow me to share a little secret - both are equally magical. I once met a wise local who said, "Sunrise is for dreamers, and sunset is for romantics." I couldn't agree more. Watching the sun paint the sky with shades of pink, gold, and lavender, you'll feel like you've been transported to a realm where time stands still.

And let's not forget the food. Oh, the food! From succulent poke bowls to the freshest catch of the day, Maui's culinary scene is a journey in itself. I still recall a meal at a seaside shack, where the scent of grilled mahi-mahi mingled with the salty breeze. Each bite was a dance of flavours, a symphony of taste that made me feel like I'd discovered a hidden treasure.

The warmth and hospitality of the locals are like a balm for the soul. I once got lost on the winding roads of Hana, only to be guided back by a kind-hearted soul who insisted on leading me to my destination.

So, as you flip through these pages, envision yourself on a journey of a lifetime. Maui is more than a destination; it's an experience. It's where adventure meets serenity, where laughter mingles with the crash of waves, and where memories are etched in the heart forever.

Welcome to Maui, dear traveller. May your days be filled with wonder, and your nights with the sweet lullabies of the Pacific. This is a place where dreams come true, and where reality surpasses even the wildest imaginings. Get ready to write your own chapter in Maui's enchanting story.

• When to Go

Choosing the right time to visit Maui can make all the difference in the world, turning a good trip into an extraordinary one. Here's a seasoned traveller's guide to the best times to experience the magic of this island paradise:

• **Weather:** Maui has a mild tropical climate year-round, with average temperatures ranging from 75-85 degrees Fahrenheit. The summer months (June-August) are typically dry and sunny, but it can get quite hot, especially in the inland areas. The winter months (December-March) are cooler and wetter, with occasional showers and the possibility of high winds and surf.

- **Crowds:** Maui is busiest during the summer months and the winter holidays. If you're looking for a more relaxed vacation, consider visiting during the shoulder seasons (April-May and September-October).

- **Budget:** Maui is a relatively expensive island, but there are ways to save money on your trip. For example, you can cook your own meals instead of eating out every night, and you can stay in a budget-friendly hostel or Airbnb instead of a resort.

Here is a summary of the best times to visit Maui for different types of travellers:

- **Families:** Summer months (June-August), when the weather is warm and sunny and there are plenty of family-friendly activities available. However, be aware that this is the busiest time of year and also means higher prices and larger crowds.

- **Couples:** Shoulder seasons (April-May and September-October), when the weather is still pleasant and there are fewer crowds.

- **Budget travellers:** Shoulder seasons (April-May and September-October), when prices for flights and accommodations are typically lower.

- **Surfers:** Winter months (December-March), when the waves are biggest and best for surfing.

- **Hikers:** Spring and fall months (April-May and September-October), when the weather is milder and there are fewer bugs.

Pro Tips:

1. Book Early: For high season and popular festivals, early reservations are key. Accommodations and activities can fill up quickly.

2. Snorkelers' Paradise: For the best underwater visibility, consider visiting in the early morning before trade winds kick in.

3. Plan for Festivals: If you're interested in cultural events, check the local calendar. Festivals like the Maui Film Festival and Aloha Festivals offer a deeper connection to the island's culture.

Ultimately, the best time to visit Maui depends on your preferences and priorities. Whether you're chasing the perfect wave, seeking solitude on a hidden beach, or immersing yourself in local festivities, Maui offers something special year-round. So, whether you're basking in the summer sun or witnessing the majesty of humpback whales, each season unveils a unique facet of this tropical paradise. Choose the time that speaks to your heart, and let Maui work its magic on your soul.

• Getting to Know Maui

Maui, often referred to as the "Valley Isle," is an enchanting slice of Hawaiian paradise nestled in the heart of the Pacific Ocean. In a nutshell, Maui is more than just an island; it's a living, breathing testament to the beauty and diversity of the natural world. It's a place where ancient traditions mingle with modern luxuries, and where every corner reveals a new facet of its boundless charm. Here's a quick guide to getting acquainted with this gem of an island:

HISTORY

Maui is the second largest island in the Hawaiian archipelago, and is known for its beautiful beaches, lush rainforests, and diverse culture. The island has a long and rich history, dating back to the Polynesian settlement of Hawaii in the 4th century AD.

The first Polynesians to arrive in Maui were likely from the Marquesas Islands, which are located about 1,500 miles to the southeast. These early settlers brought their culture and traditions with them, which helped to shape the unique Hawaiian culture that exists today.

In the 12th century, Maui was united into a single kingdom under the rule of Chief Kaka'alaneo. This kingdom lasted for over 500 years, and during that time, Maui became a centre of Hawaiian culture and learning.

In 1795, King Kamehameha I of Hawaii conquered Maui, and the island became part of the unified Kingdom of Hawaii. Kamehameha I was a skilled warrior and diplomat, and he was able to unite all of the Hawaiian Islands under his rule.

The Kingdom of Hawaii lasted until 1893, when it was overthrown by a group of American businessmen and missionaries. After the overthrow, Hawaii became a US territory, and in 1959, it became the 50th state of the United States.

Today, Maui is a popular tourist destination, and is known for its beautiful scenery, diverse culture, and friendly people. The island is also home to a number of important historical sites, such as Iao Valley State Park, where Kamehameha I defeated the Maui army in 1790.

CULTURE AND TRADITIONS

Maui is an island with a rich culture and tradition, dating back to the Polynesian settlement of Hawaii. The island's culture is a blend of Polynesian, Hawaiian, and American influences.

Here are some of the key aspects of Maui's culture and tradition:

● **Aloha spirit:** The aloha spirit is a central tenet of Hawaiian culture, and it is evident in the warm and welcoming nature of the people of Maui.

● **Respect for the land:** Hawaiians have a deep respect for the land, and they believe that it is sacred. This respect is reflected in the way that Maui residents care for their environment.

● **Family and community:** Family and community are very important in Hawaiian culture. Maui residents are known for being close to their families and friends, and they are always willing to help one another.

● **Music and dance:** Music and dance are an important part of Hawaiian culture, and they are often used to celebrate special occasions and holidays. Maui is home to a number of talented musicians and dancers, and there are many opportunities to experience Hawaiian music and dance on the island.

• **Food:** Hawaiian food is a unique and delicious blend of Polynesian, Asian, and American influences. Some of the most popular Hawaiian dishes include poke, kalua pork, and shave ice.

Here are some examples of traditional Hawaiian activities that you can experience on Maui:

• **Hula:** Hula is a traditional Hawaiian dance that is performed to tell stories and express emotions. There are many different types of hula, and you can find hula performances all over Maui.

- **Lei making:** Lei making is the art of creating leis, which are garlands of flowers or shells. Leis are often given as gifts or worn to celebrate special occasions.

- **Luau:** A luau is a traditional Hawaiian feast that features food, music, and dance. Luau is a great way to experience Hawaiian culture and cuisine.

GEOGRAPHY

Maui, aptly nicknamed the "Valley Isle," is a captivating jewel in the Hawaiian archipelago. Nestled in the Central Pacific, it spans approximately 727 square miles, making it the second-largest of the Hawaiian Islands. Its unique geography is a testament to the volcanic forces that shaped this tropical paradise.

Maui is a volcanic island, and is formed from two shield volcanoes, Haleakala and Puu Kukui.

Haleakala is the larger of the two volcanoes, and is over 10,000 feet (3,048 m) tall. Puu Kukui is the smaller of the two volcanoes, and is about 5,700 feet (1,737 m) tall.

The two volcanoes are connected by a narrow isthmus, which gives Maui its nickname, the "Valley Isle." Maui is also known for its beautiful beaches, lush rainforests, and diverse landscapes.

Here are some of the key geographic features of Maui:

1. Haleakala National Park: Haleakala National Park is home to the dormant Haleakala volcano. Haleakala is one of the largest volcanoes in the world, and its summit offers stunning views of the island.

2. Iao Valley State Park: Iao Valley State Park is a beautiful rainforest that is home to the Iao Needle, a towering rock formation.

3. Road to Hana: The Road to Hana is a scenic highway that winds along the coast of the island. The Road to Hana is known for its waterfalls, rainforests, and black sand beaches.

4. Molokini Crater: Molokini Crater is a sunken volcano that is located off the coast of Maui. It is a popular snorkelling and diving destination, due to its clear waters and diverse marine life.

Maui's geography is a symphony of contrasts, where volcanic peaks, fertile valleys, and azure coastlines converge. This diversity is a testament to the island's dynamic past, and it creates an ever-changing canvas of beauty and adventure for those fortunate enough to explore its shores. Maui's map coordinates may be fixed, but its allure is forever in flux, waiting to be discovered anew by each visitor.

• *Interesting Facts About Maui*

These fascinating facts about Maui only scratch the surface of the wonders this island holds. Each corner, whether natural or cultural, reveals a new layer of its charm and allure. Maui truly is a destination that offers something for every kind of traveller.

1. Maui is home to Haleakalā, a dormant volcano standing at over 10,000 feet (3,055 metres) tall. It offers one of the most breathtaking sunrises on Earth, often above the clouds.

2. Lahaina boasts the largest banyan tree in the United States. Planted in 1873, it now spans nearly an acre, creating a natural canopy for gatherings and events.

3. Road to Hana, this famous winding road on Maui's east coast stretches for about 52 miles (83 kilometres) and features over 600 hairpin turns and 59 bridges. It's an adventure with mesmerizing vistas at every turn.

4. Iao Needle is a defining feature of 'Iao Valley State Park, the Iao Needle is a lush, 1,200-foot (366-metre) pinnacle, rich in historical and cultural significance to the Hawaiian people.

5. Molokini Crater is a partially submerged volcanic crater off Maui's coast and is a premier snorkelling and diving destination. Its crescent shape shelters a thriving marine ecosystem.

6. Maui's waters are a favoured winter home for humpback whales. From December to April, these

magnificent creatures arrive to give birth and nurture their young.

7. Maui boasts several lavender farms, such as Ali'i Kula Lavender Farm, where visitors can wander through vibrant fields of lavender and enjoy stunning views of the island.

8. Located off the coast of Makena, Turtle Town is a well-known spot for snorkelling alongside Hawaiian green sea turtles, providing a unique and memorable underwater encounter.

9. The Seven Sacred Pools is actually a series of cascading pools in 'Ohe'o Gulch, within Haleakalā National Park, these pools are fed by waterfalls and surrounded by lush rainforest, creating a refreshing oasis.

10. In La Perouse Bay, you'll find a significant collection of petroglyphs, ancient rock carvings that offer a glimpse into Hawaii's rich cultural history.

11. Maui is also home to a number of historical churches, such as the Waiola Church and the Kaahumanu Church.

12. Maui is a popular tourist destination, but it is also a home to a thriving community of locals.

13. Maui is named after the Polynesian demigod Maui, who is credited with creating the Hawaiian Islands.

• Things To Avoid

Things to Avoid While Planning Your Trip to Maui:

1. Booking your trip too late. Maui is a popular tourist destination, so it's important to book your flights and accommodations well in advance, especially if you're travelling during the peak season (summer and winter holidays).

2. Overpacking. Maui is a casual island, so you don't need to pack a lot of clothes. Bring light, comfortable clothing and comfortable shoes, as you'll likely be doing a lot of walking.

3. Not renting a car. Maui is a relatively large island, so it's easiest to get around by car. Maui's attractions are spread out, and public transportation isn't as extensive. Don't wait until you arrive to secure a rental car; book ahead to ensure availability and

competitive rates. You can rent a car at the airport or at one of the many rental car agencies on the island.

4. Not booking activities in advance. Some popular activities, such as whale watching and snorkelling tours, can book up quickly, especially during the peak season. It's a good idea to book your activities in advance to make sure you get the dates and times you want.

5. Not packing for all types of weather. Even though Maui has a mild climate, it's always a good idea to pack for all types of weather, especially if you're planning on doing any hiking or other outdoor activities.

6. Neglecting Accommodation Reservations. Maui is a sought-after destination, especially during peak seasons. Avoid disappointment by booking

accommodations well in advance to secure your preferred lodging.

7. Overloading Your Itinerary. While Maui offers a plethora of activities, resist the temptation to over-schedule. Leave room for spontaneity and relaxation, allowing you to fully appreciate the island's natural beauty.

8. Overlooking Weather Patterns. While Maui enjoys pleasant weather year-round, it's important to be aware of occasional rain and high surf advisories, particularly during the winter months. Stay updated with local forecasts for a seamless experience.

Things to Avoid While in Maui:

1. Disrespecting the Hawaiian culture and environment. Hawaiians have a deep respect for the

land and their culture. Be sure to learn a few basic Hawaiian phrases and respect the local customs.

2. Taking lava rocks home with you. It is illegal to take lava rocks home from Hawaii. Lava rocks are considered sacred by Hawaiians, and removing them from the island can disrupt the natural ecosystem.

3. Swimming at unguarded beaches. There are many unguarded beaches on Maui, but it is important to swim only at beaches that are guarded by lifeguards. The currents and waves can be strong at some beaches, and it is important to be aware of the risks before swimming.

4. Hiking alone. If you are planning on hiking on Maui, it is important to hike with a buddy. Some of the hiking trails on Maui are challenging and can be dangerous to hike alone.

5. Drinking and driving. Hawaii has a strict DUI law, and the penalties for drinking and driving are severe. If you are planning on drinking alcohol, be sure to arrange for a designated driver.

6. Ignoring Ocean Safety. Maui's shores can have strong currents. Pay attention to posted warnings, use designated swimming areas, and consider using reef-safe sunscreen to protect the marine environment.

7. Feeding Wildlife. While it may be tempting to offer snacks to the friendly wildlife, it's best to refrain. Feeding disrupts their natural behaviours and can be harmful to their health.

8. Engaging in Off-Trail Hiking. Venturing off established trails can be dangerous and harmful to Maui's unique flora and fauna. Stick to designated

paths and respect any closures for your safety and the preservation of the environment.

9. Being Unaware of Cultural Sensitivities. Hawaii has a rich cultural heritage. Avoid trespassing on sacred sites and always ask for permission before taking photos of locals or their property.

10. Leaving Valuables in Plain Sight. While Maui is generally safe, it's best to avoid leaving valuables visible in your car. Take precautions to secure your belongings, especially when visiting popular attractions.

Travel Itinerary Planner

PART ONE: THINGS TO DO

In this section we will be looking extensively at the thrilling and fun things to do in Maui as a visitor to make sure you have a sweet and relaxing experience

• *Beaches*

Maui is home to some of the most beautiful beaches in the world, with soft white sand, crystal-clear water, and swaying palm trees. Here is a brief description of the top beaches in Maui, their locations, transportation options, activities and amenities:

1. KAANAPALI BEACH

Kaanapali Beach is a popular tourist destination, so it can be crowded, especially during the peak season. However, the beach is very long, so there is usually enough space for everyone to spread out.

• Location: West Maui, near the town of Lahaina

- Transportation: There are several bus lines that stop at Kaanapali Beach, as well as taxis and ride-sharing services.
- Activities: Swimming, sunbathing, snorkelling, surfing, paddleboarding, kayaking, and boating.
- Amenities: Lifeguards, showers, restrooms, restaurants, and shops.

2. KAPALUA BAY

Kapalua Bay is a beautiful and secluded beach with calm waters, making it a great place for families with young children.

- Location: West Maui, near the town of Kapalua
- Transportation: There is a bus line that stops at Kapalua Bay, as well as taxis and ride-sharing services.
- Activities: Swimming, sunbathing, snorkelling, and paddleboarding.

- Amenities: Lifeguards, showers, restrooms, restaurants, and shops.

3. WAILEA BEACH

Wailea Beach is a popular and upscale beach with soft white sand and clear water. The beach is also home to a number of luxury resorts and condominiums.

- Location: South Maui, near the town of Wailea
- Transportation: There are several bus lines that stop at Wailea Beach, as well as taxis and ride-sharing services.
- Activities: Swimming, sunbathing, snorkelling, surfing, paddleboarding, and kayaking.
- Amenities: Lifeguards, showers, restrooms, restaurants, and shops.

4 MAKENA BEACH

Makena Beach, also known as Big Beach, is a large and beautiful beach with soft white sand and clear water. The beach is also home to a number of sea turtles, so it is a great place to see these amazing creatures.

- Location: South Maui, near the town of Makena
- Transportation: There are a few bus lines that stop near Makena Beach, but it is easiest to get to the beach by car.
- Activities: Swimming, sunbathing, snorkelling, and surfing.
- Amenities: Lifeguards, showers, and restrooms.

5. BALDWIN BEACH PARK

Baldwin Beach Park is a popular spot for locals and tourists alike. The beach is known for its good waves and body surfing conditions.

- Location: North Maui, near the town of Paia
- Transportation: There are several bus lines that stop at Baldwin Beach Park, as well as taxis and ride-sharing services.
- Activities: Swimming, sunbathing, surfing, bodysurfing, and fishing.
- Amenities: Lifeguards, showers, restrooms, picnic tables, and barbecues.

6. HO'OKIPA BEACH PARK

Ho'okipa Beach Park is a world-famous windsurfing and kitesurfing spot. The beach offers stunning views of sunrise or sunset.

- Location: North Maui, near the town of Haiku
- Transportation: There are a few bus lines that stop near Ho'okipa Beach Park, but it is easiest to get to the beach by car.
- Activities: Windsurfing, kitesurfing, and surfing.
- Amenities: Lifeguards, showers, and restrooms.

• Watersports

Maui is a great place to enjoy a variety of water sports, from surfing and swimming to snorkelling and diving. Here is a list of some of the most popular water sports on Maui, as well as locations where you can go to do them:

1. SURFING

Surfing can be dangerous, especially if you are a beginner. It is important to take a surf lesson from a qualified instructor before surfing on your own.

- Locations: There are many surf spots on Maui, including: Hookipa Beach Park, Lahaina Harbor, Maliko Gulch, Honolua Bay and Kanaha Beach Park.
- Contact details: There are a number of surf schools and rental shops on Maui. For a list of surf schools and rental shops, visit the website of the

Maui Visitors Bureau.
https://www.gohawaii.com/islands/maui

2. SWIMMING

It is important to swim only at beaches that are guarded by lifeguards, and to be aware of the currents and waves.

- Locations: There are many beaches on Maui where you can swim, including: Kaanapali Beach, Kapalua Bay, Wailea Beach, Makena Beach, Baldwin Beach Park
- Contact details: There are lifeguards on duty at most of the popular beaches on Maui.

3. SNORKELLING

When snorkelling, it is important to wear a mask, snorkel, and fins. It is also important to be aware of marine life and not to touch or remove any sea creatures.

• Locations: There are many great snorkelling spots on Maui, including: Molokini Crater, Turtle Town, Kapalua Bay, Makena Landing and Ahihi-Kinau Natural Area Reserve.

• Contact details: There are a number of snorkel tour operators on Maui. For a list of snorkel tour operators, visit the website of the Maui Visitors Bureau.

4. DIVING

Diving can be dangerous, especially if you are not certified. It is important to dive with a qualified dive operator.

• Locations: There are many great dive spots on Maui, including: Molokini Crater, Lanai Cathedrals, Marine Life Conservation District, Turtle Town and Maluaka Beach.

• Contact details: There are a number of dive shops on Maui. For a list of dive shops, visit the website of the Maui Visitors Bureau.

5. PADDLEBOARDING

Paddleboarding is a relatively easy sport to learn, and it's a great way to explore the coastline and get some exercise.

• Locations: Many beaches and lakes on Maui are suitable for paddleboarding, including: Kaanapali Beach, Kapalua Bay, Wailea Beach, Makena Beach and Baldwin Beach Park.

• Contact details: There are a number of paddleboard rental shops on Maui. For a list of paddleboard rental shops, visit the website of the Maui Visitors Bureau.

6. KAYAKING

Kayaking is a great way to explore the coastline and see marine life.

- Locations: Many beaches and lakes on Maui are suitable for kayaking, including: Kaanapali Beach, Kapalua Bay, Wailea Beach, Makena Beach and Baldwin Beach Park.
- Contact details: There are a number of kayak rental shops on Maui. For a list of kayak rental shops, visit the website of the Maui Visitors Bureau.

7. JET SKIING

Jet skiing is a fun and exciting way to explore the coastline and get an adrenaline rush. However, it is important to be aware of the safety risks and to follow all safety instructions.

- Locations: There are a number of jet ski rental shops on Maui, located at various beaches and marinas around the island.

8. PARASAILING

Parasailing is a great way to get a bird's-eye view of the coastline and the surrounding islands. It is also a relatively safe activity, but it is important to choose a reputable tour operator.

- Locations: Parasailing tours are offered from a number of beaches and marinas around Maui. For a list of parasailing tour operators, visit the website of the Maui Visitors Bureau.

9. WINDSURFING

Windsurfing is a challenging sport to learn, but it can be very rewarding. It is important to take lessons from a qualified instructor before windsurfing on your own.

- Locations: Popular windsurfing spots on Maui include: Ho'okipa Beach Park, Kanaha Beach Park and Maalea Harbor. There are a number of windsurfing schools and rental shops on Maui. For a list of windsurfing schools and rental shops, visit the website of the Maui Visitors Bureau.

10. KITESURFING

Kitesurfing is an even more challenging sport to learn than windsurfing. It is important to take lessons from a qualified instructor before kitesurfing on your own.

- Locations: Popular kitesurfing spots on Maui include: Ho'okipa Beach Park and Kanaha Beach Park. There are a number of kitesurfing schools and rental shops on Maui. For a list of kitesurfing schools and rental shops, visit the website of the Maui Visitors Bureau.

11. BANANA BOATING AND TUBE RIDING

Banana boating and tube riding are fun and exciting activities for all ages. However, following safety instructions is essential for a safe and enjoyable experience.

• Locations: Banana boating and tube riding tours are offered from a number of beaches and marinas around Maui. For a list of banana boating and tube riding tour operators, visit the website of the Maui Visitors Bureau.

12. FISHING

A fishing licence is required to fish in Maui waters. Fishing licences can be purchased online or at most sporting goods stores on Maui.

• Locations: Fishing can be done from shore or from a boat. There are a number of fishing charters available on Maui. For a list of fishing charters, visit the website of the Maui Visitors Bureau.

13. WHALE WATCHING

Whale watching is a great way to see humpback whales and other marine life. Whale watching tours are typically offered during the winter months, when humpback whales migrate to Maui to mate and calve.

• Locations: Whale watching tours are offered from a number of beaches and marinas around Maui. For a list of whale watching tour operators, visit the website of the Maui Visitors Bureau.

You can also book boat tours to explore the coastline and visit nearby islands.

Maui is a great place to enjoy water sports because of its warm climate, clear waters, and diverse coastline. There are many different places to go for each activity, and there are also a number of tour operators that offer lessons and rentals.

Here are some additional tips for choosing the right water sport for you:

• Consider your skill level and experience. Some water sports, such as surfing and diving, require more skill and experience than others.

• Think about what you want to see and do. If you want to see marine life, snorkelling and diving are great options. If you want to get some exercise, kayaking and paddleboarding are good choices.

• Factor in the cost. Some water sports, such as jet skiing and parasailing, can be more expensive than others.

• Ask for recommendations from the locals and tour operators as well.

• Hiking and Nature

Maui is a hiker's paradise, with trails to suit all levels of experience. From easy strolls along the coast to challenging treks through the rainforest, there is a trail for everyone on Maui.

Here are a few of the most popular hiking trails on Maui:

1. Pipiwai Trail: This 4-mile trail leads to Waimoku Falls, also known as the Seven Sacred Pools. The trail is relatively easy, but the last 0.5 miles is steep and slippery.

2. Iao Valley State Monument: This easy 1-mile trail leads to the Iao Needle, a towering rock formation that is sacred to the Hawaiian people.

3. Sliding Sands Trail: This 11-mile trail leads to the bottom of Haleakala Crater. The trail is steep and challenging, but the views from the bottom of the crater are worth it.

4. Waihee Ridge Trail: This 4.7-mile trail offers stunning views of the West Maui coastline and the Haleakala Crater. The trail is moderately challenging, with occasional steep climbs.

5. Kapalua Coastal Trail: This 3.5-mile trail winds along the coast of Kapalua Bay. The trail is easy and offers beautiful views of the ocean and the surrounding islands.

Here are some expert recommendations and advice for hiking on Maui:

- Start early in the morning to avoid the heat and the crowds.
- Bring plenty of water and sunscreen.
- Wear sturdy hiking shoes or boots.

- Be aware of the weather conditions and dress accordingly.
- Let someone know where you are going and when you expect to be back.

Here are some contact information for hiking tour operators on Maui:

- Maui Hiking Adventures: (808) 270-4453
- Backroads Hawaii: (808) 242-7626
- Hiking Maui: (808) 244-4445

Here are some other necessary information for hiking on Maui:

- A hiking permit is required for the Pipiwai Trail and the Sliding Sands Trail. Permits can be secured online or in person at the trailhead.
- Some trails on Maui are closed during certain times of the year due to weather conditions or

wildlife nesting. Be sure to check the website of the Hawaii Department of Land and Natural Resources before you go.

• Be respectful of the Hawaiian people and their culture. Do not leave any trash on the trails and avoid disturbing any plants or animals.

• Haleakala National Park

Haleakala National Park is located on the island of Maui in Hawaii. The park is home to the dormant Haleakala volcano, which last erupted in 1790. The park also includes a variety of other ecosystems, such as rainforest, desert, and alpine tundra.

To get to Haleakala National Park, you can fly into Kahului Airport (OGG) on Maui. From the airport, you can rent a car and drive to the park entrance. The drive takes about one hour, thirty minutes.

There are a variety of activities to do in Haleakala National Park, including:

1. Hiking: There are over 30 miles of hiking trails in the park, ranging from easy to challenging. Some popular trails include the Pipiwai Trail, the Sliding Sands Trail, and the Halemau'u Trail.

2. Biking: You can bike down the Haleakala Crater Road or explore the Kipahulu District.

3. Camping: There are two campgrounds in the park, one in the summit area and one in the Kipahulu District.

4. Stargazing: Haleakala National Park is one of the best places in the world to go stargazing. The park offers ranger-led stargazing programs on most nights.

5. Sunrise viewing: Many people visit Haleakala National Park to watch the sunrise from the summit of Haleakala Crater. The views from the summit are breathtaking.

The cost to enter Haleakala National Park is $30 per vehicle or $15 per person on foot or bicycle. The park also offers a variety of passes, such as the America the Beautiful Pass, which is valid for one year and grants admission to all National Park Service sites.

Here are some other necessary information for tourists visiting Haleakala National Park:

• The weather in Haleakala National Park can vary greatly, so it is important to be prepared for all types of weather. It is a good idea to bring a jacket, raincoat, and sunscreen.

• The altitude at the summit of Haleakala Crater is over 10,000 feet, so it is important to acclimatize to the altitude before hiking or biking.

• *Road to Hana*

The Road to Hana is a scenic highway that winds along the coastline of Maui. The road is 64 miles long and takes about three hours to drive without stopping. Along the way, there are numerous waterfalls, rainforests, and black sand beaches to explore.

To get to the Road to Hana, you can fly into Kahului Airport (OGG) on Maui. From the airport, you can rent a car and drive to the town of Paia. The Road to Hana begins in Paia and be prepared for a leisurely drive, as the road is winding and dotted with numerous scenic stops.

Here are some of the things you can see and do along the Road to Hana:

1. Twin Falls: This waterfall is located just a few miles from Paia. This spot is known for its swimming and picnicking opportunities.

2. Hanawi Falls: This waterfall is located about 12 miles from Paia. It is a short hike from the road and is a great place to take a dip in the pool at the bottom of the falls.

3. Waimoku Falls: This waterfall is located about 22 miles from Paia. This spot is known for its swimming and cliff jumping opportunities.

4. Kipahulu District: This district is located at the end of the Road to Hana. It is home to the Pipiwai Trail, which leads to Waimoku Falls and the Pools of Ohe'o.

5. Pools of Ohe'o: These pools are also known as the Seven Sacred Pools. They are a sacred place to the Hawaiian people and are a popular spot for swimming and picnicking.

Here are some necessary information for tourists visiting the Road to Hana:

- The Road to Hana is a narrow and winding road, so it is important to drive carefully.

- There are many one-lane bridges along the road, so be prepared to yield to oncoming traffic.

- There are many stops along the road, so it is a good idea to start early in the morning to avoid the crowds.

• Begin your trip early in the morning to make the most of the day. This also allows you to beat the crowds at popular attractions.

• Fill your gas tank in Paia, as gas stations along the route are limited. Pay attention to the little things, they can make a big difference.

• Consider using a reliable GPS device or a navigation app that offers offline maps. Cellular service can be patchy on the journey.

• Bring sunscreen, bug spray, rain jackets, snacks, water, and a fully charged camera. You'll want to capture the beauty at every turn.

• Wear sturdy, waterproof shoes if you plan on exploring waterfall areas or hiking trails.

- Research and prioritize stops beforehand. Highlights include Twin Falls, Waikamoi Ridge Trail, and Wai'anapanapa State Park.

• Historic Lahaina

Historic Lahaina is a charming town on the west coast of Maui. The town was once the capital of the Hawaiian Kingdom and is now a popular tourist destination. Historic Lahaina is home to a variety of historic buildings, shops, restaurants, and art galleries.

To get there, from Kahului, take the Honoapiilani Highway (HI-30) for a scenic 25-mile (40-kilometre) drive. Alternatively, many tour companies offer guided excursions to Lahaina from various points on the island.

Here are some of the things you can see and do in Historic Lahaina:

1. Banyan Court Park: This park is home to a massive banyan tree that is over 150 years old. The park is a popular spot for people watching and picnicking.

2. Baldwin Home Museum: This museum is housed in the former home of missionary doctor Dwight Baldwin. The museum offers tours of the house and exhibits on the history of Lahaina and the Hawaiian Islands.

3. Old Lahaina Courthouse: This courthouse was built in 1859 and is now a museum. The museum offers tours of the courthouse and exhibits on the history of the Hawaiian Kingdom.

4. Lahaina Arts Society Gallery: This gallery showcases the work of local artists. The gallery offers free admission and is open to the public.

5. Front Street: This street is lined with shops, restaurants, and art galleries. A place where you can find everything from high-end boutiques to casual eateries.

6. Lahaina Jodo Mission: Experience tranquillity at this Buddhist temple with its serene gardens and striking 12-foot Buddha statue.

7. Lahaina Harbor: Watch fishing boats come and go, or embark on a sunset cruise to experience the coast from a different perspective.

8. Whalers Village Museum: Immerse yourself in Lahaina's whaling history. The museum vividly illustrates the town's days as a bustling whaling port.

Here are some other necessary information for tourists visiting Historic Lahaina:

- Historic Lahaina is a walkable town, so it is easy to get around on foot.
- Lahaina offers limited parking, especially during peak hours. To secure a spot, consider arriving early or taking public transportation.
- Historic Lahaina is a popular tourist destination, so it is a good idea to visit during the off-season to avoid the crowds.
- Visit Lahaina in the early evening to experience the sunset over the Pacific Ocean, a sight that has captivated generations of visitors
- The best way to explore Lahaina is on foot. Wear comfortable shoes for strolling along Front Street and exploring its historic sites.

• *Luau Dinner Shows*

Luaus are a great way to experience Hawaiian culture and cuisine. A luau is a traditional Hawaiian feast that typically includes food, music, and dancing. Luau dinner shows are a popular tourist attraction in Maui, and there are a number of different luaus to choose from.

Here are some of the most popular luau dinner shows in Maui:

1. Old Lahaina Luau: This luau is located in Historic Lahaina and offers a variety of cultural activities, including lei making, coconut husking, and hula dancing. The luau also features a traditional Hawaiian feast and a live band.

2. Te Au Moana Luau: This luau is located at the Wailea Beach Marriott Resort & Spa and offers a variety of cultural activities, including lei making, coconut husking, and imu ceremonies. The luau also features a traditional Hawaiian feast and a live band.

3. Myths of Maui Luau: This luau is located at the Royal Lahaina Resort and offers a variety of cultural activities, including lei making, coconut husking, and fire dancing. The luau also features a traditional Hawaiian feast and a live band.

The cost of a luau dinner show in Maui varies depending on the luau and the type of seating you choose. However, most luaus cost between $150 and $250 per person.

Luau dinner shows typically last about three hours. They typically begin with a cocktail hour, followed by a cultural performance and a traditional Hawaiian feast. The feast is usually served buffet-style and includes a variety of Hawaiian dishes, such as poi, kalua pork, and lomi salmon. After the feast, there is usually more live entertainment and dancing.

Here are some other things to keep in mind when attending a luau dinner show in Maui:

- Reservations are required for all luaus.
- It is a good idea to arrive early to get a good seat.
- Many luaus offer transportation from your hotel.
- Bring a camera to capture all of the memories.

Here are the contact details for some of the luau dinner shows in Maui:

- Old Lahaina Luau: (808) 667-6289
- Te Au Moana Luau: (808) 891-6271
- Myths of Maui Luau: (808) 879-3311
- Drums of the Pacific Luau: (808) 242-2784
- Maui Nui Luau at Black Rock: (808) 669-6222

• *Golfing*

Maui is a golfer's paradise, with over 13 golf courses to choose from. The courses range from championship layouts to affordable public courses, so there is something for everyone. Here are my personal top 5:

Here are a few of the most popular golf courses on Maui:

1. Kapalua Golf Club: This club features two world-class courses, the Plantation Course and the Bay Course. The Plantation Course has hosted the PGA Tour's Sentry Tournament of Champions since 1999. You can contact them on (808) 669-9000.

2. Wailea Golf Club: This club features three courses, the Blue Course, the Gold Course, and the Emerald Course. The Blue Course is one of the most challenging courses in Hawaii and has hosted the LPGA Tour's LOTTE Championship since 2014. You can contact them on (808) 879-1922.

3. Pukalani Country Club: This public course is a popular choice for both locals and tourists. The course offers stunning views of the Haleakala Crater and the West Maui Mountains. You can contact them on (808) 878-3000.

4. Maui Nui Golf Club: This public course is located in Kihei and offers affordable green fees. The course is famous for its challenging layout and breathtaking views of the Pacific. You can contact them on (808) 874-0777.

5. The Dunes at Maui Lani: This public course is located in Kahului and offers a unique golfing experience. The course is built on natural dune terrain and features challenging greens and fairways. You can contact them on (808) 873-0422.

Here are some other necessary information for tourists visiting Maui:

• Most golf courses on Maui require reservations. It is a good idea to make reservations in advance, especially if you are travelling during the peak season.

• Golf courses on Maui typically have dress codes. Be sure to check the dress code before you book your tee time.

• Golf courses on Maui rent clubs, but it is a good idea to bring your own clubs if you have them.

The cost of golfing on Maui varies depending on the course and the time of year. Resort courses are typically more expensive than public courses. However, many courses offer discounts for twilight rounds and early morning rounds.

Resort Courses	Free Public Courses
Kapalua Plantation Course Kapalua Bay Course Wailea Gold Course Wailea Emerald Course Wailea Blue Course Makena Golf Course The Dunes at Maui Lani Kaanapali Royal Course Kaanapali Kai Course	Maui Nui Golf Club Pukalani Country Club Kahili Golf Course The King Kamehameha Golf Club Waiehu Golf Course

• *Shopping*

Maui is a great place to shop, with a variety of stores and markets to choose from. Whether you're looking for souvenirs, clothing, or home goods, you're sure to find what you're looking for on Maui.

Here are some of the most popular shopping destinations on Maui:

1. Queen Ka'ahumanu Center: This mall is located in Kahului and is the largest mall on Maui. It features a variety of stores, including Macy's, Nordstrom, and Victoria's Secret.

2. The Shops at Wailea: This upscale shopping centre is located in Wailea and features a variety of luxury brands, including Gucci, Louis Vuitton, and Prada.

3. Whalers Village: This outdoor shopping centre is located in Ka'anapali and features a variety of shops, restaurants, and art galleries.

4. Lahaina Cannery Mall: This indoor shopping mall is located in Lahaina and features a variety of shops, restaurants, and a movie theatre.

5. Maui Arts & Cultural Center: This cultural centre is located in Kahului and features a variety of shops that sell Hawaiian art and crafts.

Here are some of the most popular markets on Maui:

1. Maui Swap Meet: This flea market is held every Saturday and Sunday at the Maui Arts & Cultural Center. It features a variety of vendors selling everything from souvenirs to clothing to food.

2. Upcountry Farmers Market: This farmers market is held every Saturday in Kula. It features a variety of vendors selling fresh produce, flowers, and prepared foods.

3. Kihei Farmers Market: This farmers market is held every Tuesday and Friday in Kihei. It features a variety of vendors selling fresh produce, flowers, and prepared foods.

4. Lahaina Farmers Market: This farmers market is held every Wednesday in Lahaina. It features a variety of vendors selling fresh produce, flowers, and prepared foods.

Be ready to haggle at these flea markets and bring a reusable bag, as many stores charge for bags.

Here are some of the things you can shop for on Maui:

- Souvenirs: Maui has a variety of souvenirs to choose from, including Hawaiian shirts, leis, and ukuleles.

- Clothing: Maui has a variety of clothing stores to choose from, including high-end boutiques and casual beachwear shops.

- Home goods: Maui has a variety of home goods stores to choose from, including stores that sell Hawaiian-themed home décor and stores that sell high-end home furnishings.

- Food: Maui has a variety of food stores to choose from, including supermarkets, specialty food stores, and farmers markets.

• Nightlife

Maui has a vibrant nightlife scene, with something to offer everyone. Whether you're looking for a lively dance club or a relaxed lounge, you're sure to find the perfect spot to let loose and have some fun.

Here are a few of the best places to party at night in Maui:

SOUTH MAUI

- **Monkeypod Kitchen:** This popular restaurant and bar has a lively atmosphere and a great selection of cocktails. Musical entertainment is also offered nightly.
- **Mama's Fish House:** This upscale restaurant and bar has a more relaxed atmosphere, but it's still a great place to enjoy a few drinks and some good company.

KIHEI

- **Tin Roof Maui:** This casual restaurant and bar has a great selection of local beers and cocktails. Musical entertainment is also offered nightly.

- **Coconut's Fish Cafe:** This popular seafood restaurant also has a lively bar scene. They often have live music and DJs on the weekends.

- **Mulligans on the Blue:** This upscale restaurant and bar has a stunning ocean view and a lively atmosphere. Musical entertainment is also offered nightly.

LAHAINA

- **Flatbread Company:** This casual restaurant and bar has a great selection of wood-fired pizzas and pastas. They also have a full bar with a variety of local beers and cocktails.

- **The Dirty Monkey:** This nightclub is one of the most popular spots to party in Lahaina. They have a large dance floor and a variety of DJs playing all night long.

- **Three's Bar & Grill:** This lively bar has a great selection of drinks and a fun atmosphere. Musical entertainment is also offered nightly.

• Art Galleries and Museums

Maui is home to a diverse range of art galleries and museums, showcasing everything from traditional Hawaiian crafts to contemporary masterpieces. Whether you're a seasoned art lover or just browsing for something to catch your eye, you're sure to find something to your taste on this beautiful island.

Here are a few of the most popular art galleries and museums on Maui:

1. Maui Arts & Cultural Center: This vibrant cultural centre in Kahului hosts a variety of art exhibitions throughout the year, featuring both local and international artists. It also has a permanent collection of Hawaiian art and artefacts.

• Opening hours: Tuesday-Saturday 10am-4pm

• Cost: Free admission

2. Hui No'eau Visual Arts Center: This nonprofit arts centre in Makawao offers a variety of art classes and workshops, as well as a rotating exhibition gallery. It also has a beautiful sculpture garden that's open to the public.

- Opening hours: Tuesday-Saturday 10am-4pm
- Cost: Free admission

3. Lahaina Arts Society Gallery: This gallery in Lahaina features a variety of works by local artists, including paintings, photography, and sculptures. It also offers art classes and workshops.

- Opening hours: Monday-Saturday 10am-5pm
- Cost: Free admission

4. Baldwin Home Museum: This historic home in Lahaina was once home to missionary doctor Dwight Baldwin and his family. Today, it's a museum that offers tours of the home and exhibits on the history of Lahaina and the Hawaiian Islands.

- Opening hours: Tuesday-Saturday 10am-4pm
- Cost: $10 for adults, $7 for children

5. Wo Hing Temple Museum: This historic temple in Lahaina was built in 1912 and is one of the oldest Chinese temples in Hawaii. Today, it's a museum that offers tours of the temple and exhibits on the history of Chinese immigration to Hawaii.

- Opening hours: Daily 9am-4pm
- Cost: $5 for adults, $2.50 for children

Other necessary information:

- Many art galleries and museums on Maui offer discounts for seniors, military members, and students.
- Be sure to check the websites of the galleries and museums you're interested in visiting before you go, as their hours may vary.

- Some galleries and museums may require reservations for tours or workshops.
- Be respectful of the artwork and follow the instructions of the staff.

• Festivals and Events

Here is a list of some of the most popular festivals and events in Maui.

1. Maui Oceanfront Marathon: January (date varies). This world-class marathon takes runners along the scenic Kaanapali Coast.

2. Great Maui Whale Festival: February (date varies). This festival celebrates the humpback whales that migrate to Maui each winter. There are whale watching tours, educational programs, and cultural events.

3 Lahaina Whale and Ocean Arts Festival: March (date varies). This festival celebrates the marine life and culture of Maui. There are art exhibits, live music, and food vendors.

4. Banyan Tree Birthday Party: April (date varies). This festival celebrates the historic Banyan Court Park in Lahaina. There are live music, food vendors, and family-friendly activities.

5. Lei Day: May 1. This holiday celebrates the Hawaiian lei, a traditional symbol of love and friendship. There are lei making demonstrations and lei competitions throughout the island.

6. Maui Arts & Cultural Center Presents: Year-round events. The Maui Arts & Cultural Center hosts a variety of events throughout the year, including concerts, plays, and dance performances.

7. East Maui Taro Festival: June (date varies). This festival celebrates the taro plant, a staple food crop in Hawaii. There are taro tastings, cooking demonstrations, and cultural events.

8. Kapalua Wine & Food Festival: June (date varies). This festival celebrates the best of Maui's food and wine scene. There are wine tastings, cooking demonstrations, and dinners prepared by celebrity chefs.

9. Maui County Fair: October (date varies). This family-friendly fair features rides, games, food vendors, and live entertainment.

10. Christmas in Lahaina: November-December (date varies). Lahaina transforms into a winter wonderland during the Christmas season. There are holiday-themed events and decorations throughout the town.

These are just a few of the many festivals and events that take place in Maui each year. With so much to see and do, you're sure to have a memorable trip no matter what time of year you visit.

• *Parks and Gardens*

Maui is home to a variety of parks and gardens, from lush rainforests to manicured botanical gardens. Whether you're looking for a place to relax and enjoy the scenery, or you're interested in learning more about Hawaiian plants and culture, you're sure to find a park or garden that's perfect for you.

Here are a few of the most popular parks and gardens in Maui:

1. Haleakala National Park: This national park is home to Haleakala, a dormant volcano with a massive crater. Located at 35589 Hana Highway, Kula, HI 96790 the park also features a variety of hiking trails, picnic areas, and scenic viewpoints.l. Cost includes $30 per vehicle, $15 per person on foot or bicycle. Contact them on (808) 572-4400.

2. Maui Tropical Plantation: Located at 1670 Honoapiilani Hwy, Wailuku, HI 96793 this plantation offers tours of its working pineapple fields, as well as a variety of other activities, such as a luau, a train ride, and a maze. The plantation also has a gift shop and a restaurant. Cost include $15 for adults, $10 for children ages 3-11, children under 3 are free. Contact them on (808) 244-7643.

3. Kula Botanical Garden: Located at 4520 Kula Hwy, Kula, HI 96790 this botanical garden features a variety of plants from all over the world, as well as a number of unique gardens, such as a Japanese garden and a succulent garden. The garden also has a number of walking paths and trails that visitors can explore. They offer a diverse selection of educational programs and events throughout the year. Cost includes $12 for adults, $6 for children ages 6-12, children under 6 are free. Contact them on (808) 276-7171.

4. Maui Ocean Center: Located at 1928 Makawao Street, Maalaea, HI 96793 this aquarium features a variety of exhibits on marine life, as well as a tropical garden that is home to a variety of Hawaiian plants. Cost include $45 for adults, $22.50 for children ages 3-12, free for children under 3. Contact them on (808) 270-7000.

5. Iao Valley State Monument: This scenic park is home to the Iao Needle, a towering rock formation that is sacred to the Hawaiian people. Located at Iao Valley Road, Wailuku, HI 96793 the park also features a walking trail that leads to a pool at the base of the Iao Needle. Cost includes $5 for adults, free for children under 12. Contact them on (808) 243-5354.

• *Family-Friendly* Activities

Maui is a beautiful island with a variety of family-friendly activities to offer visitors of all ages. Here are a few of my most popular choices:

1. Visit the beach: Maui has some of the most stunning beaches in the world, with soft white sand and crystal-clear water. Some of the most popular family-friendly beaches include Ka'anapali Beach, Kapalua Beach, and Makena Beach.

2. Go swimming: The waters around Maui are perfect for swimming, and there are many lifeguard-protected beaches to choose from. If you're looking for a more adventurous swim, you can try snorkelling or scuba diving.

3. Take a surfing lesson: Surfing is a popular activity on Maui, and there are many surf schools that offer lessons for all ages and skill levels.

4. Visit the Maui Ocean Center: This aquarium is home to a variety of marine life, including sharks, turtles, and rays. Visitors can explore and discover through interactive exhibits and educational programs.

5. Go whale watching: Maui is a great place to go whale watching, as humpback whales migrate to the island's waters every winter. There are many whale watching tours available, and you can also see whales from shore at certain locations.

6. Take a hike: Maui has a variety of hiking trails to choose from, ranging from easy to challenging. Some popular family-friendly hikes include the

Pipiwai Trail, the Iao Valley Trail, and the Kapalua Coastal Trail.

7. Visit a luau: A luau is a traditional Hawaiian feast that features food, music, and dancing. It's a great way to experience Hawaiian culture and have a fun-filled evening with your family.

8. Go ziplining: Ziplining is a thrilling activity that allows you to soar through the air while attached to a cable. There are several zipline companies on Maui that offer tours for all ages.

9. Take a helicopter tour: A helicopter tour is a great way to see the island from a different perspective. You'll see stunning views of the coastline, waterfalls, and rainforests.

10. Visit a farm: There are several farms on Maui that offer tours and activities for families. You can learn about Hawaiian agriculture, meet the animals, and even sample some of the fresh produce.

11. Go shopping: Maui has a variety of shops to choose from, including boutiques, art galleries, and souvenir shops. You can find everything from unique Hawaiian gifts to high-end fashion.

12. Dine out: Maui has a variety of restaurants to choose from, including fine dining establishments, casual eateries, and food trucks. You can find everything from Hawaiian cuisine to international fare.

• *Kids Friendly Activities*

Maui is a great place to visit with kids, with a variety of activities to keep them entertained. From exploring the beach to visiting the zoo to hiking through the rainforest, there's something for everyone on Maui.

Here are a few of the most popular kid-friendly activities on Maui:

1. Visit the beach: Maui has some of the most beautiful beaches in the world, with soft sand and clear water. Kids will love swimming, building sandcastles, and playing in the waves.

2. Go to the zoo: The Maui Ocean Center is a great place to learn about marine life. Kids will love seeing sharks, turtles, dolphins, and other creatures up close.

3. Go hiking: Maui has a variety of hiking trails, ranging from easy to challenging. There are trails that lead to waterfalls, pools, and other scenic spots.

4. Visit a farm: There are a few farms on Maui that offer tours and activities for kids. Kids can learn about where their food comes from and see animals like cows, pigs, and goats.

5. Take a surfing lesson: Surfing is a popular activity on Maui, and there are a number of surf schools that offer lessons for kids. Surfing is a great way to get exercise and have fun at the same time.

6. Go whale watching: Maui is a great place to go whale watching, especially during the winter months. There are a number of whale watching tours available, and kids will love seeing these majestic creatures up close.

7. Visit a luau: A luau is a traditional Hawaiian feast that features food, music, and dancing. Luaus are a great way to learn about Hawaiian culture and have fun at the same time.

8. Visit Maui Ocean Center: Located in Ma'alaea, this renowned marine park offers an up-close encounter with Hawaii's vibrant underwater world. Kids can marvel at sharks, sea turtles, and a wide array of marine life.

9. Iao Valley State Park: A short drive from Wailuku, this lush valley is an excellent spot for an easy family hike. The paved path leads to the iconic Iao Needle, a natural wonder for kids to discover.

10. Maui Tropical Plantation: Located in Wailuku, this working plantation offers a tram tour through acres of tropical fruit fields. Kids can learn about exotic fruits and enjoy a taste of freshly picked produce.

11. Lahaina Banyan Court: A visit to Lahaina's Banyan Court is like stepping into a natural wonderland. Kids can explore the expansive banyan tree's twisting roots and branches, providing hours of imaginative play.

Here are some other tips for planning a kid-friendly trip to Maui:

• Choose a hotel or resort that is family-friendly. Many hotels and resorts on Maui offer amenities such as kids' clubs, swimming pools, and playgrounds.

• Pack plenty of sunscreen, hats, and sunglasses for your kids. The sun can be strong in Maui, so it's important to protect your kids from the sun.

• Bring plenty of snacks and drinks for your kids. Food and drinks can be expensive on Maui, so it's a good idea to bring your own.

• Take breaks throughout the day. Kids can get tired easily, so it's important to take breaks throughout the day to rest and recharge.

• Be flexible with your plans. Things don't always go according to plan when travelling with kids, so it's important to be flexible.

• Solo Traveler Activities

Maui is a great destination for solo travellers, with a variety of activities to suit all interests. Whether you're looking to relax on the beach, explore the rainforest, or try new adventures, you're sure to find something to your liking on Maui.

Here are a few ideas for solo traveller activities in Maui:

1. Go for a hike. Maui has a variety of hiking trails to choose from, ranging from easy to challenging.

Some popular trails include the Pipiwai Trail, the Sliding Sands Trail, and the Waihee Ridge Trail.

2. Visit the beach. Maui is home to some of the most beautiful beaches in the world. Some popular beaches include Ka'anapali Beach, Kapalua Bay, and Wailea Beach.

3. Take a surfing lesson. Maui is a great place to learn how to surf. There are a number of surf schools on the island that offer lessons for all skill levels.

4. Go snorkelling or diving. Maui is home to a variety of marine life, making it a great place to snorkel or dive. There are a number of tour operators that offer snorkelling and diving excursions.

5. Visit a luau. A luau is a traditional Hawaiian feast that features food, music, and dancing. It's a great way to experience Hawaiian culture and meet new people.

6. Take a cooking class. Learn how to make some of your favourite Hawaiian dishes in a cooking class. There are a number of cooking schools on the island that offer classes for all skill levels.

7. Visit a museum or art gallery. Maui has a number of museums and art galleries to choose from. Some popular options include the Maui Arts & Cultural Center, the Hui No'eau Visual Arts Center, and the Baldwin Home Museum.

8. Take a day trip. Maui has a number of nearby islands that are perfect for a day trip. Some popular options include Molokai, Lanai, and Kahoolawe.

PART TWO: AMAZING PLACES TO VISIT

Maui has lots of beautiful and amazing places where visitors and tourists alike can explore. In this section we will be looking at a few of the top places in maui that promise to captivate every traveller's heart:

• *Haleakala Crater*

Perched atop Maui like a celestial crown, Haleakalā Crater is a geographical marvel that commands reverence. Haleakala Crater is one of the most awe-inspiring natural wonders in the world. Located on the island of Maui in Hawaii, Haleakala is a dormant volcano that rises over 10,000 feet above sea level. The crater itself is seven miles wide and two miles deep, and it's home to a variety of unique and beautiful landscapes.

Haleakala National Park is located about 20 miles from the town of Kula. There are a few different ways to get to the park, including:

- **Driving:** If you're renting a car, the best way to get to Haleakala is to drive. The drive from Kula takes about 30 minutes.
- **Taking a tour:** There are a number of tour operators that offer tours to Haleakala National Park. Tours typically include transportation to and from the park, as well as a guided tour of the crater.
- **Biking:** If you're feeling adventurous, you can bike to Haleakala National Park. The bike ride is about 36 miles round-trip and takes about 6 hours.

The best time to visit Haleakala Crater is during the spring or fall, when the weather is mild. Summers can be hot and dry, while winters can be cold and windy. Arriving before dawn is a revelation. The pre-dawn hours bring forth a celestial spectacle as the sun paints the horizon in hues of gold and crimson. Be sure to check sunrise times and plan your visit accordingly, as this is an immensely popular experience. Upon reaching the summit, a profound sense of tranquillity envelops you. The crater sprawls before you, revealing a vast, barren expanse punctuated by cinder cones and alien-like silversword plants.

There are a variety of things to do at Haleakala Crater, including:

1. Hiking: There are a number of hiking trails in the crater, ranging from easy to challenging. Some popular trails include the Sliding Sands Trail, the Halemau'u Trail, and the Pipiwai Trail.

2. Biking: You can also bike in the crater, but be sure to wear a helmet and bring plenty of water.

3. Stargazing: Haleakala Crater is a great place to stargaze, thanks to its dark skies and high elevation. If you're visiting during the summer, be sure to attend one of the ranger-led stargazing programs.

4. Watching the sunrise: Haleakala Crater is known for its stunning sunrises. If you're planning on watching the sunrise, be sure to leave early in the morning, as the drive to the summit takes about 30 minutes.

Haleakala Crater is a must-see for any visitor to Maui. With its stunning scenery, diverse wildlife, and unique cultural significance, Haleakala is a truly unforgettable place.

Additional tips to help you have a lifetime experience:

• If you're planning on watching the sunrise, be sure to make reservations in advance. Reservations can be made online or by calling the Haleakala National Park Visitor Center. +1 808-572-4400 | www.nps.gov/hale

• If you're visiting during the winter, be sure to dress warmly. The summit temperature can be freezing or below freezing.

• If you're planning on hiking to the bottom of the crater, be sure to start early in the morning. It can take up to 8 hours to hike to the bottom and back.

• Be sure to check the weather forecast before you go. The weather at Haleakala Crater can change quickly, so it's important to be prepared.

• Iao Valley State Park

Iao Valley State Park is a beautiful and sacred place located in Central Maui. The park is home to the Iao Needle, a towering rock formation that is a significant cultural landmark to the Hawaiian people. The park also features a lush rainforest, waterfalls, and a variety of native Hawaiian plants and animals. This park has been mentioned quite a few times already in the previous sections and that's because it is a highly recommended destination in Maui for a truly unforgettable experience. When you reach the Iao Needle, you will be rewarded with stunning views of the valley below. The needle is a truly sacred place to the Hawaiian people, and it is easy to understand why. The energy in the valley is palpable.

Iao Valley State Park is located in Central Maui, just west of the town of Wailuku. The park is easily accessible by car, and there is a large parking lot located at the entrance. Visitors can also take public transportation to the park, as the Maui Bus Route 35 stops directly in front of the park entrance.

The best time to visit Iao Valley State Park is during the dry season, which runs from May to October. The dry season is characterized by If you're looking for a less crowded experience, consider visiting the park during the dry season. Early mornings offer a tranquil atmosphere, as the valley awakens with the soft glow of dawn. Weekdays tend to be less crowded, providing a more serene experience. Avoiding weekends and holidays ensures a quieter visit.

• Contact details: Iao Valley State Park 367 Iao Valley Road Wailuku, HI 96793. Call (808) 248-4421.

Other necessary information that a tourist needs to know:

•The park is open daily from 7:00 AM to 6:00 PM. The park is free to enter.

- There is a paved walking path that leads to the Iao Needle. The walk is approximately 0.6 miles round trip.
- The park also has a picnic area and a restroom.
- I recommend wearing comfortable shoes and clothing when visiting Iao Valley State Park. The walking path to the Iao Needle can be slippery, so it is important to wear good shoes.
- If you are visiting the park with children, be sure to keep an eye on them at all times. There are some steep drop-offs near the walking path.

• Molokini Crater

Molokini Crater is a partially submerged volcanic crater located just off the coast of Maui, Hawaii. It is one of the most popular snorkelling and diving destinations in the world, and for good reason. The crater's crystal-clear waters and abundant marine life offer visitors a chance to experience the underwater world in a truly unforgettable way.

Molokini Crater is located about 2.5 miles off the coast of Makena State Park in South Maui. The only way to get to Molokini Crater is by boat. There are a number of tour companies that offer snorkelling and diving excursions to the crater, and most depart from Maalaea Harbor. Tour boats typically depart from Maalaea Harbor in the morning and return in the afternoon. The boat ride to Molokini Crater takes about 45 minutes.

Another option is to charter a private boat to Molokini Crater. This is a good option for groups or families who want more flexibility. However, it is important to note that chartering a boat can be more expensive than taking a tour boat.

The best time to visit Molokini Crater is during the summer months (May-September), when the weather is calm and the water visibility is at its best. However, Molokini Crater is a year-round destination, and it is possible to snorkel or dive there at any time of year. Molokini's prime time for snorkelling and diving is early morning when the sea conditions are typically calm, visibility is excellent, and marine life is most active. Booking a morning tour ensures you'll experience the crater at its finest.

When you arrive at Molokini Crater, you will be given a safety briefing and snorkelling or diving gear. Once you are in the water, you will be amazed by the clarity of the water and the abundance of marine life.

Molokini Crater is home to over 250 species of fish, including colourful parrotfish, angelfish, and butterflyfish. You may also see sea turtles, eels, and octopus.

If you are a certified diver, you can explore the deeper waters of Molokini Crater. The outside wall of the crater drops off to a depth of over 300 feet, and there is a variety of marine life to see, including sharks, rays, and dolphins.

Here are the contact details for a few tour companies that offer snorkelling and diving excursions to Molokini Crater:

- Maui Snorkel Tours: (808) 879-3681
- Pride of Maui: (808) 242-2784
- Redline Rafting: (808) 875-4446

My extra Recommendations:
- **Snorkelling Gear:** While many tours provide equipment, consider bringing your own mask and snorkel for a comfortable and personalized experience.

- **Underwater Camera:** Don't forget to capture the mesmerizing marine life and the stunning underwater landscapes. Waterproof cameras are invaluable for preserving your memories.

- **Motion Sickness Prevention:** If you're prone to seasickness, consider taking precautions before boarding. Ginger candies or wristbands can be effective remedies.

• Makena State Park

Makena State Park is a beautiful and popular state park located in South Maui, Hawaii. It is home to two stunning beaches: Big Beach and Little Beach. Big Beach is known for its expansive white sand beach and large waves, while Little Beach is known for its secluded cove and calm waters.

Makena State Park is located about 10 miles south of Wailea and 20 miles south of the Kahului Airport

(OGG). To get to the park by car, take Highway 31 south to Makena Road. Turn right onto Makena Road and follow it to the park entrance.

There is also a public bus that stops at the park entrance. The bus ride from Kahului Airport to Makena State Park takes about 1 hour and 45 minutes. The best way to get around Makena State Park is on foot or by bike. There is a paved walking/biking path that runs along the coast and connects the two beaches. There is also a parking lot at each beach.

The best time to visit Makena State Park is during the shoulder season (April-May and September-October), when the weather is mild and there are fewer crowds. The park can be crowded during the summer months, especially on weekends and holidays.

Other necessary information you need to know:

- There is a $10 parking fee at Makena State Park.

- There are restrooms and showers at each beach.

- There are no lifeguards on duty at Makena State Park.

My Recommendations and advice:

- If you are visiting Makena State Park during the summer months, try to arrive early in the morning to avoid the crowds.

- If you are planning on swimming at Big Beach, be aware of the strong currents. It is best to swim in the lifeguard-protected area.

- If you are visiting Little Beach, be aware that it is a popular nude sunbathing spot.

- Be sure to respect marine life and the environment. Do not disturb any plants or animals, and take all of your trash with you.

- If you are interested in hiking, there is a short trail that leads to the top of Pu'u Olai (Little Beach Crater). The hike offers stunning views of the coast and the Haleakala volcano.

- There are also a number of picnic areas at Makena State Park. If you are planning on having a picnic, be sure to bring a blanket and plenty of food and drinks.

- Makena State Park is a great place to watch the sunset. Don't miss out on capturing the unforgettable views with your camera.

- While Makena's beaches are inviting, always exercise caution and adhere to posted warnings, especially during periods of high surf or strong currents. Don't forget to keep an eye on the little ones if you are visiting with family.

- Contact details: Makena State Park 100 Makena Road Kula, HI 96753 Call (808) 984-8164.

• Waihee Ridge Trail

The Waihee Ridge Trail is one of the most popular hikes on Maui, and for good reason. It offers stunning views of the West Maui Mountains, the Pacific Ocean, and the Waihee Valley. The trail is also relatively easy to access and moderate in difficulty, making it a great option for hikers of all levels.

The Waihee Ridge Trail is located in the West Maui Mountains, about a 20-minute drive from the town of Lahaina. To get to the trailhead, take Highway 30 west to the town of Waihee. Turn left onto Kahekili Highway and follow it for about 5 miles. The trailhead will be on your right, just past the Camp Maluhia BSA sign. There are a few public transportation options available, even though private transportation is not. The Maui Bus Route 30 runs from Lahaina to Waihee, and there is a stop near the trailhead. There are also a number of taxi and shuttle companies that operate on Maui.

The best time to hike the Waihee Ridge Trail is during the spring or fall, when the weather is mild. Summers can be hot and humid, and winters can be wet and muddy.

Other necessary information you should know:

- The Waihee Ridge Trail is a 4-mile round-trip hike. It takes about 2-3 hours to complete.
- The trail is well-maintained, but there are some steep sections.
- Be sure to wear comfortable shoes and clothing, and bring plenty of water and sunscreen.
- There are no restrooms at the trailhead, so be sure to use the restroom before you start your hike.
- Dogs are allowed on the trail, but they must be on a leash.

My recommendations and advice:

• Consider starting your hike early in the day to catch the stunning morning light filtering through the trees and to avoid potential midday crowds.

• While the trail is navigable on your own, guided tours often provide valuable insights into the local flora, fauna, and cultural significance of the area.

• Don't miss out on capturing the unforgettable views with your camera.

• Take your time and enjoy the hike. There is no need to rush.

• Be aware of your surroundings and watch your step, especially on the steep sections of the trail.

• For additional information or updates, consider contacting the Maui Office of Tourism. Maui Land & Parks Department (808) 270-7389

• If you are planning to hike the Waihee Ridge Trail during the peak season (December-March), be sure to arrive early to find a parking spot. The trailhead parking lot is small and can fill up quickly.

• If you are hiking with children, be sure to keep a close eye on them. Steep drop-offs can be dangerous. Watch your footing carefully along the trail.

• If you are hiking during the winter, be sure to dress for all types of weather. The mountain weather can be unpredictable. Be prepared for all conditions, and turn back if the weather deteriorates.

• *Bamboo Forest*

The bamboo forest of Maui is a magical place. It is located in the Kipahulu District of Haleakala National Park, on the eastern side of the island. The forest is made up of thousands of towering bamboo stalks, some of which reach up to 100 feet tall. The bamboo stalks are so dense that they block out the sun, creating a cool and shady environment.

The best way to experience the bamboo forest is to hike the Pipiwai Trail. The trail is 2 miles long and round-trip, and it takes about an hour to complete. The trail is mostly flat and easy to walk, but there are a few sections where it can be slippery. The trail culminates at Waimoku Falls, a cascading waterfall that plunges 400 feet (122 meters) into a tranquil pool. It's a breathtaking sight and a perfect reward for your trek.

To get to the bamboo forest, you will need to drive to the Kipahulu District of Haleakala National Park. The drive takes about 2 hours from Lahaina and 3 hours from Kahului. There is a parking lot at the trailhead, and there is also a shuttle bus that runs from the parking lot to the start of the trail.

The best time to visit the bamboo forest is during the spring or fall, when the weather is mild. The climate is characterized by hot, humid summers and cold, rainy winters. Visit in the early morning to revel in the forest's serene atmosphere before the day's crowds arrive. The sun's rays filtering through the bamboo culms create a magical ambiance that's not to be missed. Be aware of your surroundings. The bamboo forest is a popular spot for wild pigs, so it is important to be aware of your surroundings and make noise as you walk to avoid startling them. Wear sturdy, closed-toe shoes for the hike, and bring plenty of water. Additionally, consider packing a rain jacket, as the weather in this area can be unpredictable.

• Ali'i Kula Lavender Farm

Ali'i Kula Lavender Farm is a breathtaking oasis nestled on the slopes of Haleakala volcano on the island of Maui. The farm is home to over 55,000 lavender plants and 20 different varieties of lavender, creating a vibrant and fragrant landscape that will enchant your senses.

As you approach the farm, the sweet aroma of lavender will greet you and instantly transport you to a place of tranquillity and serenity. The farm's winding paths lead you through fields of lavender, where you can stop and admire the beauty of the plants and breathe in the calming scent.

The farm also features a variety of other attractions, including a lavender distillery, a gift shop, and a tearoom. In the distillery, you can learn about the process of extracting lavender essential oil and see firsthand how the farm's lavender products are made. The gift shop offers a wide selection of lavender-themed products, including soaps, lotions, candles, and culinary items. And the tearoom serves up delicious lavender-infused treats and beverages, such as lavender scones, lavender tea, and lavender lemonade.

Ali'i Kula Lavender Farm is located in the Upcountry region of Maui, about 45 minutes from Kahului Airport. The farm is accessible by car, taxi, or tour bus. If you are renting a car, the easiest way to get to Ali'i Kula Lavender Farm is to drive. The farm is located at 4520 Kula Highway, Kula, HI 96790. If you are not renting a car, you can take a taxi or tour bus to the farm. There are a number of taxi companies and tour operators that offer transportation to Ali'i Kula Lavender Farm.

The best time to visit Ali'i Kula Lavender Farm is during the lavender blooming season, which runs from June to September. However, the farm is open year-round, and the lavender plants are always beautiful.

Other necessary information you need to know:

• The farm is open daily from 10am to 4pm.

- Admission is $3 for adults, $1 for children ages 6-12, and free for children under 6.
- There is a gift shop and tearoom on site.
- The farm is accessible by wheelchair.
- Pets are not allowed on the farm.

Here are a few recommendations and invaluable advice for planning your visit to Ali'i Kula Lavender Farm:

- Go early in the morning or late in the afternoon to avoid the crowds and the heat.
- Wear comfortable shoes and clothing, as you will be doing a lot of walking.
- Take your time and enjoy the beauty of the lavender fields.
- Be sure to visit the lavender distillery and gift shop.
- Try some of the delicious lavender-infused treats and beverages at the tearoom.

- Don't forget your camera! The vibrant colours, serene landscapes, and stunning vistas are a photographer's dream.
- Contact details Phone: (808) 878-3004
  Website: www.aliikulalavender.com

• *Maui Ocean Center*

The Maui Ocean Center is a world-class aquarium located in Ma'alaea, Maui, Hawaii. It is the largest living tropical reef aquarium in the Western Hemisphere and is home to a variety of marine life, including sharks, turtles, tropical fish, and coral reefs.

The Maui Ocean Center is located on the west coast of Maui, just off of Highway 31. It is about a 15-minute drive from the town of Kihei and a 30-minute drive from the town of Lahaina.

There are a number of transportation options available to visitors to the Maui Ocean Center. Visitors can drive their own car, take a taxi or ride-sharing service, or take a shuttle bus. Shuttle buses are available from a number of hotels and resorts on Maui.

The best time to visit the Maui Ocean Center is during the off-season (April-May and September-October), when the crowds are smaller and the weather is cooler. The Maui Ocean Center is open year-round, but it is important to note that some exhibits and activities may be closed during the off-season.

Things to See and Do:

The Maui Ocean Center offers a variety of exhibits and activities for visitors of all ages. Some of the most popular exhibits include:

1. Open Ocean: This exhibit features a variety of marine life, including sharks, turtles, and tropical fish. Visitors can walk through a transparent tunnel to get a close-up view of the animals.

2. Humpback Whale Habitat: This exhibit features a life-size model of a humpback whale. Visitors can learn about the biology and behaviour of humpback whales and see how they migrate to Maui each winter.

3. Turtle Lagoon: This exhibit features a variety of sea turtles, including green sea turtles and hawksbill sea turtles. Visitors can learn about the different types of sea turtles and see how the Maui Ocean Center is helping to conserve these endangered animals.

4. Touch Pool: This exhibit allows visitors to touch and interact with a variety of marine life, including sea stars, sea urchins, and hermit crabs. It is a great way for children to learn about the ocean and its inhabitants.

In addition to its exhibits, the Maui Ocean Center also offers a variety of activities for visitors, including:

1. Animal Encounters: Visitors can have a close-up encounter with a variety of marine animals, including sharks, turtles, and penguins.

2. Behind-the-Scenes Tours: Visitors can take a behind-the-scenes tour to learn about the Maui Ocean Center's operations and to see how the aquarium takes care of its animals.

3. Educational Programs: The Maui Ocean Center offers a variety of educational programs for visitors of all ages. These programs teach visitors about the ocean and its inhabitants.

My recommendations and advice:

• Purchase your tickets in advance to avoid long lines.

• Aim for an early morning visit to beat the crowds and enjoy a peaceful exploration of the exhibits. Weekdays also tend to be quieter than weekends

• Wear comfortable shoes and clothing, as you will be doing a lot of walking.

• Be respectful of marine life and the environment. Do not touch the animals or disturb the exhibits.

Contact Details: Maui Ocean Center 192 Ma'alaea Road Ma'alaea, HI 96793 Call (808) 270-7000

• Bailey House Museum

The Bailey House Museum is a must-see for any visitor to Maui. Located in the historic town of Wailuku, the museum is housed in a beautiful 19th-century home that was once the residence of missionary Samuel and Mary Bailey. Today, the museum offers visitors a glimpse into the lives of the early missionaries and the Hawaiian people they served.

The museum's collection includes a variety of Hawaiian artefacts, including tools, weapons, and clothing. Visitors can also learn about the history of the Hawaiian Islands and the Hawaiian monarchy. The museum's educational programs and events engage visitors of all ages all year round.

The Bailey House Museum is located at 2375A Main Street, Wailuku, HI 96793. The museum isn't difficult to locate as you can get there by car or public transportation.

If you are driving, take Highway 30 to Wailuku. The museum is located on the right-hand side of the road, just before the intersection of Main Street and Vineyard Street. If you are taking public transportation, take the Maui Bus to the Wailuku Post Office stop. The museum is located a short walk from the bus stop.

The Bailey House Museum is open year-round, but the best time to visit is during the spring or fall when the weather is mild. The museum is also less crowded during these months.

The Bailey House Museum is open Tuesday through Friday from 10am to 2pm. Admission is $10 for adults, $7 for seniors, and $4 for children ages 6-12. Children under 6 are free.

Here are a few recommendations and invaluable advice for visiting the Bailey House Museum:

- Take your time and enjoy the exhibits. The museum has a lot to offer, so be sure to set aside enough time to see everything.
- Be sure to check out the museum's gift shop. The gift shop sells a variety of Hawaiian-themed souvenirs, including books, jewelry, and clothing.
- If you are interested in learning more about Hawaiian culture, be sure to attend one of the museum's educational programs or events.
- The museum is also a great place to take photos. Be sure to bring your camera and capture all of the beautiful sights.

The Bailey House Museum can be reached at (808) 244-3326. You can also visit the museum's website at https://mauimuseum.org/.

• La Perouse Bay

La Perouse Bay, also known as Keoneʻōʻio Bay, is a hidden gem on the southern coast of Maui. It is a rugged and beautiful area with lava rock cliffs, black sand beaches, and stunning views of the Pacific Ocean.

La Perouse Bay is located at the end of Makena Alanui Road, about 10 miles south of Wailea. The road to La Perouse Bay is paved but narrow and winding. It is important to drive carefully and be aware of the sharp lava rocks.

There are a few different ways to get to La Perouse Bay:

• Drive: This is the most common way to get to La Perouse Bay. There is a parking lot at the end of Makena Alanui Road, but it can fill up quickly, especially on weekends and holidays.

- Take a tour: There are a number of tour companies that offer tours to La Perouse Bay. This is a good option if you want to learn more about the area from a knowledgeable guide.
- Hike: There is a hiking trail that leads to La Perouse Bay from the Ahihi-Kinau Natural Area Reserve. This is a challenging hike, but it offers stunning views of the coastline.

The best time to visit La Perouse Bay is during the summer months (May-September), when the weather is warm and sunny. However, it is important to be aware that the area can be windy, so it is a good idea to bring a jacket or sweater.

Other necessary information you should know:

- La Perouse Bay is a popular spot for swimming, sunbathing, snorkelling, and fishing. However, it is important to be aware of the strong currents and riptides.

- There are no lifeguards on duty at La Perouse Bay, so it is important to swim with caution.
- There are no restrooms or other facilities at La Perouse Bay, so it is important to come prepared.

Activities and Recommendations:

1. Hiking and Exploration: The King's Highway Trail, a historical route once used by Hawaiian royalty, offers a captivating hike along the shoreline. Be sure to wear sturdy, closed-toe shoes and bring plenty of water.

2. Snorkeling and Diving: The bay's crystal-clear waters reveal a thriving underwater world. Bring snorkel gear and explore the vibrant coral reefs, teeming with tropical fish and marine life. Exercise caution near sharp lava formations.

4. Wildlife Watching: Keep an eye out for Hawaiian spinner dolphins and green sea turtles, which frequent the bay. Give them plenty of space and watch them from a safe distance.

5. Picnicking and Relaxation: There are no amenities in the immediate area, so it's advisable to pack a picnic lunch and plenty of water. Enjoy your meal while soaking in the panoramic views of the bay.

• Contact details: Maui County Parks & Recreation: (808) 270-7389

Additional recommendations:

• If you are interested in learning more about the history and culture of La Perouse Bay, be sure to visit the Pu'u Pehe Historical Park. This park features a number of interpretive signs and exhibits that tell the story of the people who have lived in the area over the centuries.

• If you are looking for a unique dining experience, be sure to make a reservation at the Mama's Fish House restaurant. This restaurant is located right on the water and offers stunning views of La Perouse Bay.

• *Waianapanapa State Park*

Waianapanapa State Park is a 122-acre state park located on the Hana Highway in East Maui. The park is known for its black sand beach, sea caves, blowholes, and lush rainforest.
Waianapanapa State Park is located at 3500 Hana Highway, Hana, HI 96713. It is about 53 miles east of Kahului, the main airport on Maui.

There are a few ways to get to Waianapanapa State Park:

1. **By car:** The best way to get to the park is by car. The drive from Kahului takes about 1 hour and 30 minutes.

2. **By bus:** There is a public bus that runs from Kahului to Hana. The bus stop for Waianapanapa State Park is located at the entrance to the park.

3. **By tour:** There are a number of tour companies that offer day trips to Hana, including stops at Waianapanapa State Park.

Once you arrive at Waianapanapa State Park, you can get around the park on foot. There is a paved walkway that leads to the black sand beach, sea caves, blowholes, and other features of the park.

The best time to visit Waianapanapa State Park is during the summer months (June-August) when the weather is warm and sunny. However, the park can be crowded during this time of year. If you are looking for a more relaxed experience, consider visiting the park during the shoulder season (April-May and September-October). Additionally, visiting on a weekday may offer a more serene experience compared to weekends.

Other necessary information you should know:

• There is an admission fee to Waianapanapa State Park. Admission is free for Hawaii residents and children under 3. For non-residents, admission is $10 for adults and $5 for children ages 3-12.
• The park is open daily from 7am to 6pm.
• The park has a number of facilities, including restrooms, picnic tables, and a gift shop.
• The park is accessible to visitors with disabilities. There is a paved walkway that leads to the black

sand beach, sea caves, blowholes, and other features of the park.

My recommendations and advice:

- The park can get crowded, especially during the summer months. Arriving early in the morning will help you avoid the crowds and enjoy the park in peace.
- There are no food or drink vendors in the park, so be sure to bring water with you.
- Waianapanapa State Park is a beautiful place, so be sure to leave no trace.
- Contact details: (808) 248-4821
- The coastal trail is a must-do. It leads to hidden coves, sea arches, and lava tubes, offering unique perspectives of the coastline.
- Bring along a picnic, as the park offers several shaded areas with picnic tables. Enjoying a meal

with the sound of crashing waves as your backdrop is an unforgettable experience.

• While the black sand beach is captivating, it's important to exercise caution when swimming due to potentially strong currents. Always follow posted warnings and lifeguard instructions.

What to do in Waianapanapa State Park:

1. Swim at the black sand beach: Waianapanapa State Park is known for its black sand beach, which is created from lava that has been eroded over time. The black sand beach is a beautiful place to relax and swim.

2. Visit the sea caves: Waianapanapa State Park has a number of sea caves that you can explore. The sea caves are formed by waves crashing against the lava cliffs.

3. See the blowholes: Waianapanapa State Park has a number of blowholes, which are natural openings in the lava rock that allow seawater to shoot into the air.

4. Hike through the rainforest: Waianapanapa State Park is home to a lush rainforest. There are a number of hiking trails that you can take to explore the rainforest.

5. Visit the Pools of Ohe'o: The Pools of Ohe'o, also known as Seven Sacred Pools, are located a short drive from Waianapanapa State Park. The Pools of Ohe'o are a series of waterfalls and pools that are sacred to the Hawaiian people.

• *Lahaina Historic District*

Lahaina Historic District is a charming town located on the west coast of Maui. The town was once the capital of the Hawaiian Kingdom and is now a popular tourist destination. Lahaina Historic District is home to a variety of historic buildings, shops, restaurants, and art galleries.

Lahaina Historic District is located about 20 minutes west of Kahului Airport (OGG). The best way to get to Lahaina from Kahului Airport is by car. Alternatively, you can also take a taxi or a shuttle bus if you are on a budget.

The best way to get around Lahaina Historic District is on foot. The compact town is easy to explore on foot, or you can rent a bicycle or take a horse-drawn carriage ride for a unique perspective.

The best time to visit Lahaina Historic District is during the shoulder seasons (April-May and September-October). The weather is pleasant and less crowded during these months.

Other necessary information you should know:

1. Lahaina Historic District is a popular tourist destination, so it's important to book your accommodations in advance, especially if you're traveling during the peak season.

2. There are a variety of restaurants in Lahaina Historic District, serving everything from Hawaiian cuisine to international fare.

3. Lahaina Historic District is home to a variety of shops, selling everything from souvenirs to clothing to home goods.

4. There are a number of art galleries in Lahaina Historic District, showcasing the work of local artists.

My recommendations and advice:

- Be sure to visit the Banyan Court Park. This park is home to a massive banyan tree that is over 150 years old. The park is a popular spot for people watching and picnicking.

- Take a walk down Front Street. This street is lined with shops, restaurants, and art galleries. A thriving commercial district with a mix of independent and chain businesses, as well as ample seating for people-watching.

- Visit the Baldwin Home Museum. This museum is housed in the former home of missionary doctor Dwight Baldwin. The museum offers tours of the house and exhibits on the history of Lahaina and the Hawaiian Islands.

- Visit the Old Lahaina Courthouse. This courthouse was built in 1859 and is now a museum. The museum offers tours of the courthouse and exhibits on the history of the Hawaiian Kingdom.

- Attend a luau. A luau is a festive Hawaiian celebration that showcases traditional cuisine, music, and dance. It's a unique opportunity to immerse yourself in Hawaiian culture and connect with others.

• *Napili Bay*

Napili Bay is a crescent-shaped bay located on the northwest coast of Maui, Hawaii. It is known for its stunning white sand beach, clear blue waters, and lush green mountains. Napili Bay is a popular destination for tourists and locals alike, and it is a great place to relax and enjoy the natural beauty of Maui.

Napili Bay is located about 15 minutes north of Lahaina and 30 minutes north of Kapalua. The best way to get to Napili Bay is by car. There are also a number of taxi and shuttle companies that offer transportation to and from Napili Bay. Once you arrive in Napili Bay, you can get around on foot or by bicycle.

The best time to visit Napili Bay is during the summer months (May-October), when the weather is warm and sunny. However, Napili Bay is a beautiful place to visit year-round.

Napili Bay is a great place to relax and enjoy the natural beauty of Maui. Here are a few of the things you can do in Napili Bay:

- Swim in the clear blue waters
- Sunbathe on the white sand beach
- Snorkel and see a variety of marine life
- Hike in the lush green mountains
- Visit the Napili Bay Resort, which offers a variety of amenities, including a restaurant, bar, and spa
- Play golf at the Kapalua Bay Resort, which is located nearby

- Contact details: Napili Bay Resort: (808) 669-6271

• *Hanauma Bay Nature Preserve*

Hanauma Bay Nature Preserve is a world-renowned marine sanctuary located on the southeastern coast of Maui, Hawaii. This bay spot is a favourite for snorkelling, swimming, and sunbathing. The bay is home to a variety of marine life, including tropical fish, sea turtles, and coral reefs.

Hanauma Bay Nature Preserve is located about 30 minutes from Lahaina and 45 minutes from Kahului Airport. There are a number of ways to get to the bay, including:

1. **By car:** The best way to get to Hanauma Bay Nature Preserve is by car. You need to worry about where to park as there is a large parking lot at the entrance to the park.

2. By bus: The Maui Bus offers service to Hanauma Bay Nature Preserve. Visitors can take bus number 22 from Lahaina or bus number 23 from Kahului Airport.

3. By taxi or ride-sharing: Visitors can also take a taxi or ride-sharing service to Hanauma Bay Nature Preserve.

The best time to visit Hanauma Bay Nature Preserve is in the morning, when the water is calmest and the crowds are smallest. The bay is open from 7:30am to 4:00pm daily.

Other necessary information for tourists:

• **Admission fee:** There is an admission fee to enter Hanauma Bay Nature Preserve. The fee is $7.50 for adults and $3.75 for children ages 3-12. Children under 3 are free.

• **Snorkel gear:** Snorkel gear is available to rent at the entrance to the park.

- **Environmental education:** Hanauma Bay Nature Preserve is a marine sanctuary, and it is important to protect the environment. Visitors should avoid touching or standing on the coral reefs.

- **Safety:** Visitors should swim with caution and be aware of the currents.

- Contact details: Hanauma Bay Nature Preserve 7455 Hanauma Bay Road Honolulu, HI 96825 (808) 922-5813

• Hui No'eau Visual Arts Center

Hui No'eau Visual Arts Center is a non-profit arts education organization located in Makawao, Maui. The center is housed in a beautiful historic estate that was once the home of Harry Baldwin, the founder of the Maui Pineapple Company.

Hui No'eau offers a variety of art classes and workshops for all ages and skill levels. The center also has a rotating exhibition gallery that showcases the work of local artists. Hui No'eau is a great place to learn about Hawaiian art and culture, and to experience the creativity of the Maui community.

Hui No'eau is located in the town of Makawao, which is about 15 miles from Kahului Airport. The center is easily accessible by car. There is also a public bus that runs to Makawao from Kahului.

Hui No'eau is open year-round. The ideal time to visit is during the shoulder seasons of spring and fall, when the weather is pleasant and the crowds are smaller.

Hui No'eau offers a variety of amenities for visitors, including a gift shop, a cafe, and a sculpture garden. The center is also wheelchair accessible.

• Contact details: Hui No'eau Visual Arts Center
2841 Baldwin Ave, Makawao, HI 96793
(808) 572-6560

My recommendations and advice:

- Be sure to check out the rotating exhibition gallery at Hui No'eau. The gallery showcases the work of local artists, and it's a great way to learn about the Maui arts community.
- If you're interested in learning about Hawaiian art, Hui No'eau offers a variety of classes and workshops. The classes are taught by experienced artists, and they're a great way to learn new skills and techniques.
- Hui No'eau is a great place to relax and enjoy the beauty of Maui. The center has a beautiful sculpture garden and a cafe where you can grab a bite to eat.
- If you're traveling with children, Hui No'eau offers a variety of family-friendly activities. The center has a children's art studio and it offers family art classes.

Overall, Hui No'eau Visual Arts Center is a great place to visit for anyone interested in art, culture, or simply enjoying the beauty of Maui. I highly recommend visiting the center when you are on the island.

• *Ke'anae Peninsula*

Ke'anae Peninsula is a stunning finger of lava that juts out into the Pacific Ocean, located on the Road to Hana on the east coast of Maui. It is a remote and rugged area, with towering cliffs, crashing waves, and lush taro fields. The peninsula is home to a small Hawaiian village of the same name, which has been inhabited for centuries.

The Ke'anae Peninsula is located about 16 miles past Paia on the Road to Hana. To get there, simply follow the Road to Hana signs from Paia. The road is narrow and winding, so drive carefully and allow plenty of time for the journey.

The best way to get to the Ke'anae Peninsula is by car. However, if you do not have a car, you can also take a tour bus or taxi from Paia or Lahaina.

The best time to visit the Ke'anae Peninsula is during the summer months (June-August), when the weather is warm and dry. However, the peninsula is beautiful year-round, and each season offers its own unique charms.

There are a variety of things to do on the Ke'anae Peninsula, including:

1. Visit the Ke'anae Arboretum: This arboretum features a variety of native Hawaiian plants and trees.
2. Hike to Ke'anae Point: This short hike offers stunning views of the peninsula and the surrounding coastline.

3. Swim at Ke'anae Beach: This black sand beach is a popular spot for swimming and sunbathing.

4. Visit the Ke'anae Congregational Church: This historic church was built in 1856 and is a beautiful example of Hawaiian architecture.

5. Learn about Hawaiian culture: The Ke'anae Peninsula is a great place to learn about Hawaiian culture and traditions. Visitors can visit the Ke'anae Community Center to learn more about the history of the peninsula and its people.

Additional information:

• The Ke'anae Peninsula is a popular spot for photography. If you are planning on taking pictures, be sure to bring your camera and tripod.

• The Ke'anae Peninsula is also a popular spot for hiking. If you are planning on hiking, be sure to wear comfortable shoes and bring plenty of water.

- The Ke'anae Peninsula is a remote and rugged area. If you are planning on visiting, be sure to let someone know where you are going and when you expect to be back.
- Contact details: Ke'anae Community Center: (808) 248-7662.

• *Paia, Maui*

Paia is a charming town located on the north shore of Maui, Hawaii. It is known for its laid-back atmosphere, eclectic mix of shops and restaurants, and stunning natural beauty.

Paia is located about 30 minutes from Kahului Airport (OGG), the main airport on Maui. To get to Paia, you can rent a car, take a taxi, or take the Maui Bus.

Paia is a great place to visit year-round. It has lovely weather, with mostly sunny skies and mild temperatures in the mid-70s to mid-80s Fahrenheit. However, the best time to visit Paia is during the shoulder seasons (April-May and September-October), when the crowds are smaller and the weather is still pleasant.

Paia has something to offer everyone. Here are a few of the most popular things to do in Paia:

1. Shop the boutiques: Paia is home to a variety of unique boutiques and shops, selling everything from Hawaiian souvenirs to vintage clothing.

2. Dine at the restaurants: Paia has a variety of restaurants to choose from, serving everything from fresh seafood to local cuisine.

3. Visit the Maui Arts & Cultural Center: The Maui Arts & Cultural Center is located just outside of Paia and offers a variety of performances and exhibitions throughout the year.

4. Explore the Paia Bay: Paia Bay is a beautiful beach located just a short walk from the town center. Visitors can swim, sunbathe, snorkel, or simply relax on the beach.

5. Take a walk through the Paia Town Park: Paia Town Park is a small park located in the heart of the town. A perfect place to people-watch and enjoy the atmosphere.

Here are a few recommendations and advice for visiting Paia:

• Try the local food: Paia has a variety of great restaurants serving local cuisine. Be sure to try some of the local favourites, such as poke, kalua pork, and loco moco.

- Relax and enjoy the atmosphere: Paia is a laid-back town, so be sure to relax and enjoy the atmosphere. There is no need to rush in Paia.

Here are a few contact details for businesses and organizations in Paia:

- Maui Arts & Cultural Center: (808) 242-2787
- Paia Town Park: (808) 270-7353
- Paia Chamber of Commerce: (808) 249-8472

• Kula, Maui

Kula is a charming upcountry town located on the slopes of Haleakala volcano in Maui, Hawaii. It is known for its cooler temperatures, lush forests, and stunning views of the island. Kula is a popular destination for tourists and locals alike, and is home to a variety of attractions, including the Kula Botanical Garden, the Maui Tropical Plantation, and the Maui Arts & Cultural Center at the Iao Valley.

Kula is located about an hour's drive from Kahului Airport (OGG). The best way to get to Kula is by car. There are a variety of rental car companies that operate at the airport. If you are not renting a car, there are a number of taxi and shuttle companies that offer transportation to Kula.

Once you are in Kula, the best way to get around is by car. There are a number of roads that wind through the town and offer stunning views of the surrounding countryside. There is also a public bus system that serves Kula, but it is not as extensive as the bus system in other parts of Maui.

The best time to visit Kula is during the shoulder seasons (spring and fall), when the weather is mild and there are fewer crowds. The climate in this region is characterized by hot and humid summers and cool and rainy winters.

Other necessary information for tourists:

- Kula is located at a higher elevation than the coast, so be sure to wear comfortable shoes and clothing.
- Kula is a rural area, so be sure to bring sunscreen, insect repellent, and a hat.
- There are a number of restaurants and shops in Kula, but the selection is not as extensive as in other parts of Maui.
- Kula is a popular destination for birdwatching. There are a number of trails that wind through the town and offer opportunities to see a variety of native and migratory birds.

Here are a few recommendations for things to do in Kula:

1. Visit the Kula Botanical Garden: This beautiful garden is home to a variety of Hawaiian plants, including flowers, trees, and shrubs. The garden also has a number of walking paths and trails that visitors can explore.

2. Take a tour of the Maui Tropical Plantation: This working plantation grows a variety of tropical fruits, including pineapples, mangoes, and papayas. The plantation offers a variety of tours and activities, including a tram tour, a pineapple train tour, and a zipline tour.

3. Visit the Maui Arts & Cultural Center at the Iao Valley: This cultural center offers a variety of exhibits, performances, and classes. The center is also located near the Iao Needle, a towering rock formation that is a sacred site to the Hawaiian people.

4. Go for a hike in the Kula Forest Reserve: This forest reserve is home to a variety of hiking trails that offer stunning views of the surrounding countryside.

5. Visit the Kula Country Farms: This farm offers a variety of activities, including pick-your-own produce, a petting zoo, and a corn maze.

Contact details:

- Kula Botanical Garden: (808) 276-7171
- Maui Tropical Plantation: (808) 244-7643
- Maui Arts & Cultural Center at the Iao Valley: (808) 242-2787
- Kula Forest Reserve: (808) 249-4710
- Kula Country Farms: (808) 878-5844

Travel Itinerary Planner

PART THREE: WHAT AND WHERE TO EAT

Maui, with its rich agricultural heritage and diverse cultural influences, offers a tantalizing array of dining experiences. In this section we will explore some top recommendations for where to eat and what to eat in Maui.

• Must-Try Dishes

Maui's culinary scene is a vibrant tapestry of flavours, blending indigenous Hawaiian ingredients with influences from around the world. Here are some delectable dishes and cuisines that every visitor should savour:

1. Poke: Poke is a traditional Hawaiian dish made with raw fish, seaweed, and other ingredients. It is a healthy and delicious dish that is perfect for a hot Maui day.

2. Kalua pork: Kalua pork is a traditional Hawaiian dish made with pork that is cooked in an underground oven. The pork is tender and flavorful, and it is often served with poi and other Hawaiian dishes.

3. Loco moco: Loco moco is a popular Hawaiian dish made with a hamburger patty, rice, a fried egg, and brown gravy. It is a hearty and satisfying dish that is perfect for breakfast, lunch, or dinner.

4. Malasadas: Malasadas are Portuguese donuts that are popular in Hawaii. They are fried and coated in sugar, and they can be filled with custard, whipped cream, or other fillings.

5. Spam musubi: Spam musubi is a popular Hawaiian snack made with a slice of grilled Spam on top of a block of rice wrapped in seaweed. It is a convenient and delicious snack that is perfect for on the go.

6. Shave ice: Shave ice is a popular Hawaiian dessert made with shaved ice that is flavoured with syrups and topped with various toppings, such as azuki beans, whipped cream, and mochi.

In addition to these traditional Hawaiian dishes, Maui also has a variety of other cuisines to offer. Here are a few recommendations:

• **Seafood:** Maui is surrounded by water, so it is no surprise that seafood is one of the most popular cuisines on the island. There are a number of restaurants that serve fresh seafood, including fish, shrimp, and lobster.

- **Asian fusion:** Maui is home to a number of Asian fusion restaurants that serve a variety of dishes, such as sushi, poke bowls, and Thai curry.

- **Farm-to-table:** Maui is home to a number of farm-to-table restaurants that serve dishes made with fresh, local ingredients.

- **Food trucks:** Maui also has a number of food trucks that serve a variety of cuisines, including tacos, burgers, and poke bowls.

• *Recommended Restaurants*

1. Mama's Fish House: Located at 799 Poho Pl, Paia, HI 96779. Mama's Fish House is a fine-dining restaurant located on the beach in Paia. The restaurant has a romantic and elegant atmosphere, with stunning views of the ocean. The menu at Mama's Fish House features a variety of fresh seafood dishes, as well as steaks, lamb, and vegetarian options. Some of the most popular dishes include the macadamia nut-crusted mahi mahi, the grilled opakapaka, and the prime filet mignon. The average cost per meal at Mama's Fish House is around $100. You can call for reservations (808) 579-8484.

2. Merriman's Kapalua: Located at 1 Bay Dr, Kapalua, HI 96761. Merriman's Kapalua is a fine-dining restaurant located on the beach in Kapalua. The restaurant has a casual and elegant atmosphere, with stunning views of the ocean. The menu at Merriman's Kapalua features a variety of fresh seafood dishes, as well as steaks, lamb, and vegetarian options. Some of the most popular dishes include the seared scallops, the pan-roasted mahi mahi, and the Kauai lamb rack. The average cost per meal at Merriman's Kapalua is around $100. You can contact them on (808) 669-6400

3. Spago Maui: Located at 3500 Wailea Alanui Dr, Wailea, HI 96753. Spago Maui is a fine-dining restaurant located at the Four Seasons Resort Maui at Wailea. The restaurant has a modern and elegant atmosphere, with stunning views of the ocean. The menu at Spago Maui features a variety of creative and innovative dishes, made with the freshest ingredients. Some of the most popular dishes include the wood-fired pizzas, the grilled fish, and the steak tartare. The average cost per meal at Spago Maui is around $125. You can make reservations by calling (808) 874-2200.

4. Roy's Kaanapali: Located at 200 Kaanapali Pkwy, Lahaina, HI 96761. Roy's Kaanapali is a fine-dining restaurant located at the Hyatt Regency Maui Resort & Spa. The restaurant has a modern and elegant atmosphere, with stunning views of the ocean. The menu at Roy's Kaanapali features a variety of Hawaiian fusion dishes, such as the miso-glazed salmon, the macadamia nut-crusted mahi mahi, and the kalua pork. The average cost per meal at Roy's Kaanapali is around $100. You can contact them on (808) 661-1999.

5. The Restaurant at Hotel Wailea: Located at 555 Kaukahi St, Wailea, HI 96753. The Restaurant at Hotel Wailea is a fine-dining restaurant located at the Hotel Wailea. The restaurant has a romantic and elegant atmosphere, with stunning views of the ocean. The menu at The Restaurant at Hotel Wailea features a variety of fresh seafood dishes, as well as steaks, lamb, and vegetarian options. Some of the most popular dishes include the seared scallops, the grilled opakapaka, and the prime filet mignon. The average cost per meal at The Restaurant at Hotel Wailea is around $125. Book a reservation with 808) 874-2500.

Here are 5 top budget-friendly restaurants in Maui:

1. Tin Roof Maui: Casual, counter-service restaurant with a lively atmosphere. Located at 100 N. Kihei Rd., Suite 104, Kihei, HI 96753. Tin Roof Maui serves a variety of Hawaiian comfort food, including pork belly bowls, garlic noodles, and kalua pork tacos. They also have a full bar with a variety of local beers and cocktails. Average cost per meal is $15-$20. Contact detail, (808) 868-0753.

2. Fork & Salad Maui: Modern, fast-casual restaurant with a focus on healthy and sustainable food. Located at 1800 Honoapiilani Hwy, Suite 104, Kihei, HI 96753. Fork & Salad Maui serves a variety of salads, sandwiches, and bowls that are made with fresh, local ingredients. Their smoothie and juice menu features a variety of flavours and options.

Average cost per meal is $10-$15. Contact detail, (808) 879-3675.

3. Coconut's Fish Cafe: Casual, family-friendly restaurant with a beachy atmosphere. Located at 3300 Akeakamai Rd., Kihei, HI 96753. Coconut's Fish Cafe serves a variety of fresh seafood dishes, including fish tacos, shrimp scampi, and grilled mahi mahi. In addition to their main courses, they also have a variety of burgers, sandwiches, and salads to choose from, so there's something for everyone. Average cost per meal is $15-$20. Contact detail, (808) 879-2626.

4. Da Kitchen: Casual, counter-service restaurant with a local vibe. Located at 1099 Lower Main St., Wailuku, HI 96793. Da Kitchen serves a variety of Hawaiian and Asian fusion dishes, including loco moco, kalua pork tacos, and poke bowls. They also have a full bar with a variety of local beers and cocktails. Average cost per meal is $10-$15. Contact detail, (808) 249-3302.

5. Flatbread Company: Casual, family-friendly restaurant with a lively atmosphere. Located at 4299 Lower Honoapiilani Rd., Lahaina, HI 96761. Flatbread Company serves a variety of wood-fired pizzas, pastas, and salads. They also have a full bar with a variety of local beers and cocktails. Average cost per meal is $15-$20. Contact detail, (808) 661-9113.

PART FOUR: ESSENTIAL TRAVEL INFORMATION

When visiting a destination it is important to equip yourself with some vital travel information to help you have a truly unforgettable experience. So in this section we will talk about the essential things you need to know as you plan your trip of a lifetime.

• Tips for Planning Your Trip

As a seasoned traveler to Maui, I'm delighted to share some invaluable advice to help you make the most of your trip to this enchanting island. Here are some tips to ensure you have an authentic and memorable experience:

1. Choose the right time of year to visit: Maui has a great climate year-round, but there are some things to keep in mind when choosing the best time to visit. The summer months (June-August) are the busiest and most expensive time of year, but the weather is also the best. The winter months (December-February) are cooler and wetter, but there are fewer crowds and the prices are lower. The shoulder seasons (spring and fall) offer a good balance of good weather, fewer crowds, and lower prices.

2. Book your accommodations in advance: Maui is a popular tourist destination, so it is important to book your accommodations in advance, especially if you are traveling during the peak season. There are a variety of accommodations to choose from, including hotels, condos, and vacation rentals.

3. Rent a car: Maui is a large island, and the best way to get around is by car. There is a public bus system on the island, but it is not as extensive as the bus system in other parts of Hawaii.

4. Plan your activities: There are a variety of activities to choose from on Maui, including hiking, swimming, snorkelling, golfing, and shopping. Be sure to plan your activities in advance so that you can make the most of your time on the island.

5. Pack for all types of weather: Maui has a variety of microclimates, so it is important to pack for all types of weather. Be sure to bring sunscreen, a hat, and sunglasses, even if you are traveling during the winter months. You should also pack a raincoat and umbrella, especially if you are traveling during the rainy season.

6. Be respectful of Hawaiian culture: Maui is a beautiful island with a unique culture. Be sure to be respectful of the Hawaiian culture and environment when you are visiting.

7. Embrace the Aloha Spirit: Hawaii's warm and welcoming culture is a cornerstone of the island experience. Take the time to learn a few basic Hawaiian phrases and always greet locals with a warm "Aloha!"

8. Attend a Local Event or Festival: Check for local events, festivals, or cultural celebrations happening during your visit. This offers a chance to immerse yourself in Maui's vibrant traditions and connect with the local community.

9. Chase Sunset Views: Maui's sunsets are legendary. Seek out prime spots like Haleakalā Summit or Wailea Beach for breathtaking views. Don't forget your camera!

10. Support Local Businesses: Maui boasts a thriving community of artisans, farmers, and entrepreneurs. Visit local markets, dine at independent restaurants, and shop at boutique stores to support the island's economy and discover unique treasures.

• Best Places to Stay in Maui

Here are some of the best cities and towns to stay in Maui, along with their reasons, proximity to top attractions, and types of accommodation that can be found in each area:

1. **Lahaina:** Lahaina is a charming historic town on the west coast of Maui. It is known for its art galleries, boutiques, restaurants, and lively nightlife.

Proximity to top attractions: Ka'anapali Beach, Kapalua Bay, Napili Bay, Maui Ocean Center and Haleakala National Park.

Types of accommodations: Hotels, Condos and Vacation rentals.

2. Wailea: Wailea is a luxurious resort area on the south coast of Maui. It is known for its beautiful beaches, world-class golf courses, and high-end shopping.

Proximity to top attractions: Wailea Beach, Makena Beach, Ahihi-Kinau Natural Area Reserve, Maui Arts & Cultural Center and Iao Valley State Monument.

Types of accommodations: Hotels, Condos and Vacation rentals.

3. Kula: Kula is a quiet and rural town in the upcountry region of Maui. It offers stunning views of Haleakala volcano and the surrounding countryside.

Proximity to top attractions: Haleakala National Park, Kula Botanical Garden, Maui Tropical

Plantation, Upcountry Farmers Market and Maui Arts & Cultural Center at the Iao Valley

Types of accommodations: Bed and breakfasts, Vacation rentals and Cottages.

4. Paia: Paia is a charming town on the north shore of Maui. It is known for its laid-back atmosphere, eclectic shops, and art galleries.

Proximity to top attractions: Road to Hana, Ho'okipa Beach Park, Pools of Ohe'o (Seven Sacred Pools) and Waimoku Falls.

Types of accommodations: Bed and breakfasts, Vacation rentals and Cottages.

• Tour Guide Operators

Tour Guide	Contact	Price
Aloha Spirit Tours	(808) 879-2414	$100-$200
Maui Vista Tours	(808) 249-5353	$75-$150
Polynesian Adventure Tours	(808) 244-7633	$50-$100
Maui Eco Tours	(808) 249-2193	$150-$300
Trilogy Excursions	(808) 276-6161	$100-$200

Please note that these are just a few examples, and there are many other tour guides operating in Maui. Prices may vary depending on the type of tour, the duration of the tour, and the number of people in your group. It is always best to contact the tour guide directly to get an accurate quote.

• Money Saving Tips

The currency of Maui is the United States (US) dollar (USD). You can use your credit or debit cards at most businesses in Maui, but it is always a good idea to have some cash on hand, especially for smaller businesses and for tipping. You can exchange currency at most banks and currency exchange bureaus in Maui.

Here are some money matters to keep in mind when traveling to Maui:

1. Tipping: It is customary to tip in Maui, especially for good service. A standard tip is 15-20% for servers, bartenders, and taxi drivers.

2. Sales tax: The sales tax in Maui is 4.166%.

3. ATM fees: Most ATMs in Maui charge a fee for using them. Be sure to check the fee schedule before using an ATM.

4. Exchange rates: The exchange rate for foreign currencies can fluctuate, so it is important to check the exchange rate before exchanging your money.

5. Credit cards: Credit cards are widely accepted in Maui, but it is always a good idea to have some cash on hand, especially for smaller businesses and for tipping.

6. Debit cards: Debit cards are also widely accepted in Maui, but be sure to check with your bank to make sure that your debit card will work in Hawaii.

Here are some tips for saving money in Maui:

1. Eat at local restaurants: Local restaurants are often less expensive than tourist traps.

2. Take advantage of free activities: There are many free activities to enjoy in Maui, such as hiking, swimming, and sunbathing.

3. Look for discounts and coupons: Many businesses in Maui offer discounts and coupons for tourists.

4. Use public transportation: The Maui Bus system is a convenient and affordable way to get around the island.

5. Stay in a vacation rental: Vacation rentals can be a more affordable option than hotels, especially for families or groups.

By following these tips, you can save money on your trip to Maui without sacrificing your enjoyment.

• Safety Guidelines

To ensure your trip is not only enjoyable but also safe, here are some essential guidelines to keep in mind:

1. Be aware of the dangers of the ocean: Maui is a beautiful island with many beaches, but it is important to be aware of the dangers of the ocean. Strong currents, rip tides, and waves can all pose a hazard. Always swim at a lifeguarded beach and obey all warning signs.

2. Wear sunscreen: Maui has a strong sun, so it is important to wear sunscreen with an SPF of 30 or higher. Reapply sunscreen every two hours, or more often if swimming, sweating, or doing any rigorous outdoor activities.

3. Drink plenty of water: It is important to stay hydrated, especially in the hot Maui climate. I advise you to drink clean water at intervals throughout the day, even if you're not thirsty.

4. Be aware of your surroundings: Maui is a relatively safe island, but it is always important to be aware of your surroundings. I advise you to avoid walking alone at night or in dark areas and be careful and observant in crowded areas, don't be carried away or absent minded.

5. Be careful when hiking: Maui has many hiking trails, but some can be challenging. Make sure your footwear and clothing are appropriate for the conditions, and bring enough water to stay hydrated.

6. Be careful when driving: Maui has a number of winding roads, so it is important to drive carefully. Be careful at night and in bad weather, such as heavy rain, fog, or snow.

7. Wildlife Awareness: While encountering marine life is an exciting part of Maui, keep a safe distance from animals like sea turtles and monk seals. Do not touch or feed them.

8. Emergency Services: Learn and save the local emergency numbers in your phone.

Here are some necessary emergency contacts in Maui:

- 911: Police, Fire Department, and Ambulance
- (808) 244-6400: Maui County Emergency Management Agency (MEMA)
- (808) 244-7077: Maui Police Department (MPD)
- (808) 270-6500: Maui Fire Department (MFD)
- (808) 249-3691: Maui County Department of Health (MCDH)
- (808) 243-3332: Maui Memorial Medical Center (MMMC)

- (808) 270-7900: Kula Hospital

- (808) 249-2577: Hale Makua Health Services (HMHS)

- (808) 242-4144: Poison Control Center (PCC)

- (808) 248-5500: Maui Humane Society (MHS)

- (808) 270-7000: Hawaiian Electric (HECO)

- (808) 244-7000: Maui Gas Company (MGC)

- (808) 244-6400: Maui County Department of Water Supply (DWS

9. Healthcare and Medical Services: Familiarize yourself with the location of medical facilities, hospitals, and clinics on the island. Carry any necessary medications and have travel insurance for peace of mind.

Here are some healthcare and medical services in Maui, their locations, and contact details:

1. Hospitals

182

• Maui Memorial Medical Center

Location: 221 Mahalani Street, Wailuku, HI 96793

Phone: (808) 244-9056

• Kula Hospital

Location: 2681 Maui Veterans Highway, Kula, HI 96753

Phone: (808) 270-7900

2. Urgent Care Centers

Doctors On Call Maui Urgent Care Center

Location: 670 Ala Moana Boulevard, Lahaina, HI 96761

Phone: (808) 667-7676

Maui Walk-In Clinic

Location: 1819 S Kihei Road, Kihei, HI 96753

Phone: (808) 874-5500

3. Community Health Centers

Maui Community Health Center - Wailuku

Location: 54 High Street, Suite 301, Wailuku, HI 96793

Phone: (808) 984-8200

Maui Community Health Center - Lahaina

Location: 1819 W Luakini Street, Lahaina, HI 96761

Phone: (808) 667-7375

This is just a small sample of the healthcare and medical services available in Maui. For more information, you can visit the website of the Maui District Health Office or the Hawaii Department of Health.

Please note that some of these services may require insurance, so be sure to check with your provider before making an appointment.

10. Weather Preparedness: Be aware of weather conditions and potential hazards. Stay updated on forecasts, especially if you plan to engage in outdoor activities.

By adhering to these safety guidelines, you'll not only ensure a smooth and enjoyable trip but also contribute to the preservation and protection of Maui's natural and cultural heritage. Remember, safety is an integral part of having a truly memorable travel experience.

• Useful Resources

Here is a list of useful resources to help you have a seamless experience in Maui:

1. Maui Visitors Bureau: The Maui Visitors Bureau is a great resource for information on everything from attractions to dining to accommodations. You can visit their website or call them at (808) 244-3530.

2. GoHawaii.com: GoHawaii.com is the official website of the Hawaii Tourism Authority. It provides comprehensive information on all of the Hawaiian islands, including Maui.

3. Maui Now: Maui Now is a local news website that provides information on current events, weather, and traffic.

4. Snorkel Bob's: Snorkel Bob's is a local snorkel shop that offers snorkel rentals and snorkel tours.

Snorkel Bob's in Maui has six convenient locations:

• Kahana Gateway: 4405 Honoapiilani Hwy, Lahaina, HI 96761. Phone: (808) 446-3585

- Honokowai: 3350 Lower Honoapiilani Road 201, Lahaina, HI 96761. Phone: (808) 667-9999
- Lahaina: 1217 Front St, Lahaina, HI 96761. Phone: (808) 661-4421
- Azeka Store: Azeka Place II, 1279 S. Kihei Road 310, Kihei, HI 96753. Phone: (808) 875-6188
- South Kihei: Kamaole Bch. Center, 2411 S. Kihei Rd. A2, Kihei, HI 96753. Phone: (808) 879-7449
- Wailea: 100 Wailea Ike Dr, Kihei, HI 96753. Phone: (808) 874-0011

Snorkel Bob's is open daily from 7:30am to 5:30pm. They offer a variety of snorkel gear rentals, as well as guided snorkel tours and other activities

5. Boss Frog's Dive & Surf: Boss Frog's Dive & Surf is a local dive shop that offers scuba diving lessons and dive tours.

Address: 1819 S Kihei Rd, Kihei, HI 96753

Phone: (808) 874-5225

Hours: 8:00am - 5:00pm, 7 days a week

Boss Frog's is a popular dive shop and surf school in Maui. They offer a variety of services, including: Snorkel and scuba diving rentals, Surfboard rentals, Stand-up paddle board rentals, Kayak rentals, Snorkel and scuba diving tours, Surf lessons, Stand-up paddleboard lessons, Kayak lessons.

Boss Frog's is a great place to go if you are looking to rent or purchase water sports equipment, or if you are interested in taking a lesson.

6. Shaka Guide: This app provides GPS-guided audio tours of Maui, including the Road to Hana, Haleakala National Park, and Iao Valley State Monument.

7. GyPSy Guide: This app offers similar audio tours as Shaka Guide, but it also includes a variety of other features, such as offline maps and interactive quizzes.

8. Maui by Local: This app is created by a Maui local and provides recommendations on everything from restaurants and activities to beaches and hiking trails.

9. Maui Bus: This app provides real-time bus arrival information for the Maui Bus system.

10. Uber: This app is a great way to get around Maui if you don't have a car. It is also a good option for late-night transportation.

11. Lyft: This app is similar to Uber and offers another option for getting around Maui without a car.

12. ParkMobile: This app allows you to pay for parking at metered spots on Maui. It is a convenient way to avoid having to carry cash or coins.

13. SunSmart: This app provides UV index forecasts and sun protection tips. It is a great way to stay safe in the Maui sun.

14. AllTrails: This app provides information on hiking trails all over the world, including Maui. It is a great way to find new trails to explore.

• Suggested Itineraries

Here are three itineraries tailored for different types of travelers:

Romantic Weekend Getaway in Maui

Day 1
• Morning:

- Arrive in Maui and check into a romantic beachfront resort in Wailea.

- Enjoy a leisurely breakfast at the resort's ocean-view restaurant.

●Afternoon:

- Spend the afternoon lounging on the beach, or take a couples' massage at the resort's spa.

● Evening:

- Watch the sunset at Makena Beach, followed by a romantic dinner at a beachside restaurant.

Day 2

● Morning:

- Rise early for a sunrise visit to Haleakalā National Park. Don't forget to bring a blanket and warm clothes.

● Afternoon:

- Explore the charming town of Lahaina. Stroll hand-in-hand along Front Street and visit Lahaina Banyan Court.

● Evening:

- Indulge in a fine dining experience at Lahaina Grill.

7 Days Family Holiday in Maui

Day 1-3

- Maui Ocean Center:

- Explore marine life at the Maui Ocean Center in Ma'alaea.

- Beach Time:

- Spend quality time at kid-friendly beaches like Kamaole Beach Parks and Baby Beach.

- Iao Valley State Park:

- Take a family hike in Iao Valley to witness the impressive Iao Needle.

Day 4-5
- Road to Hana:
  - Embark on a family road trip along the Hana Highway, stopping at waterfalls and scenic spots.

- Hana Cultural Center:
  - Learn about Hawaiian history and culture in Hana.

Day 6-7:
- Whale Watching (Seasonal):
  - Take a whale watching tour (seasonal) to witness humpback whales in their natural habitat.

- Lahaina Historic District:
  - Explore Lahaina's historic sites, including the Banyan Tree Park and Baldwin Home Museum.

7 Days Solo Adventure in Maui

Day 1-2

- Haleakalā Summit:

  - Start your solo adventure with a sunrise visit to Haleakalā National Park. Hike or bike through the otherworldly landscape.

- Paia Town:

  - Explore the eclectic town of Paia, known for its art galleries and unique shops.

Day 3-4

- Hiking Adventure:

  - Embark on a solo hiking adventure in the West Maui Mountains or explore the Pipiwai Trail in Hana.

- Surfing or SUP:

   - Try your hand at surfing or stand-up paddleboarding in one of Maui's renowned surf spots.

Day 5-7
- Snorkeling Expedition:

  - Go on a solo snorkelling adventure at Molokini Crater or explore the underwater world at Honolua Bay.
- Farm Tour:

   - Join an agricultural tour to learn about Maui's local produce and sustainable farming practices.

- Culinary Exploration:

   - Sample the island's culinary delights at local food trucks and eateries.

Each itinerary is tailored to make the most of your time in Maui, ensuring you have a memorable experience, whether you're seeking romance, family fun, or solo adventure.

• *Essential Hawaiian Phrases*

When visiting Hawaii, knowing a few key Hawaiian phrases not only shows respect for the local culture but also enhances your experience on the islands. Here are some essential phrases to help you navigate and connect with the spirit of aloha:

1. Aloha - [ah-LO-ha]
Meaning: Hello, goodbye, love, affection, and compassion. It embodies the core value of Hawaiian culture.

2. Mahalo - [mah-HAH-loh]
Meaning: Thank you. Express your gratitude with this commonly used phrase.

3. E Komo Mai - [eh KAW-moh MY]

Meaning: Welcome. Extend a warm welcome or invitation to someone.

4. Ohana - [oh-HAH-nah]
Meaning: Family. Emphasizing the importance of family bonds.

5. Mahalo nui loa - [mah-HAH-loh NOO-ee LOH-ah]
Meaning: Thank you very much. An extra expression of gratitude.

6. A hui hou - [ah HOO-ee HO]
Meaning: Until we meet again. A farewell phrase, often used with a sense of anticipation for a future reunion.

7. Keiki - [KAY-kee]
Meaning: Child or children. Used to refer to young ones.

8. Pau - [pow]
Meaning: Finished, done, or completed. Use it to indicate that something is finished.

9. Mauka - [MOW-kah]
Meaning: Toward the mountains. Used in giving or receiving directions.

10. Makai - [mah-KAH-ee]
Meaning: Toward the ocean. Another directional term, useful for navigation.

To learn the Hawaiian language extensively or to a good extent, I will be listing some apps to help you learn seamlessly. These apps offer a variety of features, such as interactive lessons, audio recordings, and games, to help you learn Hawaiian phrases. Some of the apps also offer offline access, so you can learn while you're on the go.

Here are some apps to learn Hawaiian phrases:

Drops, Memrise, Duolingo, Rosetta Stone, Babbel, LingoDeer, Pimsleur, uTalk, Hawaiian Language App, Hawaiian Phrasebook, Hawaiian Translator.

CONCLUSION

As we draw the curtains on this Maui travel guide, we hope you're infused with a newfound sense of anticipation and wonder for the experiences that await you on the Valley Isle. Maui, with its lush landscapes, crystalline waters, and warm-hearted locals, beckons you to embark on a journey unlike any other.

From the dramatic sunrise at Haleakalā's summit to the rhythmic waves of Hana's coast, this island pulsates with a vibrant energy that leaves an indelible mark on all who venture here. The scent of plumeria flowers, the taste of fresh poke, the echo of Hawaiian melodies—these are the elements that create the symphony of Maui.

But beyond its breathtaking scenery, Maui is a treasure trove of cultural richness. Its history, deeply rooted in the ancient traditions of the Polynesian navigators, is reflected in every corner, from the Lahaina Banyan Tree to the chants of hula dancers on the beaches.

We encourage you to explore not only the well-trodden paths, but also the hidden gems that await your discovery. Engage with local artisans, savour farm-to-table delicacies, and let the waves be your lullaby as you rest under the swaying palms.

As the sun dips below the horizon, painting the sky in hues of orange and pink, know that you've witnessed a glimpse of Maui's timeless magic. It's a magic that lingers, inviting you back to these shores, time and time again.

So, with gratitude for sharing in this adventure, we bid you a fond aloha and hope that Maui has left an imprint on your soul, just as it has on ours. Until we meet again on this island of dreams, may the spirit of aloha guide your travels.

Travel Itinerary Planner

Travel Itinerary Planner

_____

_____

_____

_____

_____

_____

_____

_____

_____

_____

_____

_____

Made in United States
Troutdale, OR
01/07/2025

27686849R00116